4-31

EXECUTIVE AGREEMENTS AND PRESIDENTIAL POWER IN FOREIGN POLICY

EXECUTIVE AGREEMENTS AND PRESIDENTIAL POWER IN FOREIGN POLICY

Lawrence Margolis

PRAEGER

PRAEGER SPECIAL STUDIES • PRAEGER SCIENTIFIC

New York • Philadelphia • Eastbourne, UK
Toronto • Hong Kong • Tokyo • Sydney

Library of Congress Cataloging-in-Publication Data

Margolis, Lawrence
  Executive agreements and presidential power in
foreign policy.

  Bibliography: p.
  Includes index.
  1. United States — Foreign relations — Executive
agreements.   2. Executive power — United States.
3. United States — Foreign relations administration.
I. Title.
KF5057.M37   1985   342.73′0412   85-12484
ISBN 0-03-006078-8 (alk. paper)   347.302412

Published in 1986 by Praeger Publishers
CBS Educational and Professional Publishing, a Division of CBS Inc.
521 Fifth Avenue, New York, NY 10175 USA

Printed in the United States of America on acid-free paper

INTERNATIONAL OFFICES

Orders from outside the United States should be sent to the appropriate address listed below. Orders from areas not listed below should be placed through CBS International Publishing, 383 Madison Ave. New York, NY 10175 USA

Australia, New Zealand
Holt Saunders, Pty, Ltd., 9 Waltham St., Artarmon, N.S.W. 2064, Sydney, Australia

Canada
Holt, Rinehart & Winston of Canada, 55 Horner Ave., Toronto, Ontario, Canada M8Z 4X6

Europe, the Middle East, & Africa
Holt Saunders, Ltd., 1 St. Anne's Road, Eastbourne, East Sussex, England BN21 3UN

Japan
Holt Saunders, Ltd., Ichibancho Central Building, 22-1 Ichibancho, 3rd Floor, Chiyodaku, Tokyo, Japan

Hong Kong, Southeast Asia
Holt Saunders Asia, Ltd., 10 Fl, Intercontinental Plaza, 94 Granville Road, Tsim Sha Tsui East, Kowloon, Hong Kong

Manuscript submissions should be sent to the Editorial Director, Praeger Publishers, 521 Fifth Avenue, New York, NY 10175 USA

Published and Distributed by the
Praeger Publishers Division
(ISBN Prefix 0-275)
of Greenwood Press, Inc.,
Westport, Connecticut

To my parents,
sister, brothers,
and mentor, Dr. George Grassmuck

CONTENTS

LIST OF TABLES AND FIGURES

All tables appear in Appendix A.

TABLES

FIGURES

EXECUTIVE AGREEMENTS
AND PRESIDENTIAL POWER
IN FOREIGN POLICY

1

INTRODUCTION

Perhaps the most significantly neglected subject in the history of American foreign policy is the executive agreement.[1]

In 1963 President John Fitzgerald Kennedy told Francisco Franco, the autocratic ruler of Spain, that "a threat to either country . . . would be a matter of common concern to both," and Franco concurred.[2] This was the same Francisco Franco who had started the civil war that snuffed out democracy in Spain, the same man who had been sympathetic to Nazi Germany in World War II. Spain was not excluded from the North Atlantic Treaty Organization by accident; but John Kennedy had no qualms about throwing the U.S. blanket of protection over Spain by presidential decree. Did John Kennedy have the power to commit the United States' military might to the defense of Spain without obtaining Senate approval (two-thirds of the Senate) of a treaty?

President Kennedy's commitment to Spain undoubtedly raised some eyebrows, and many members of Congress balked at the notion; but there was no national outcry against an "imperial" president. Indeed, such an action was far from extraordinary in the U.S. foreign policy arena. As precedents, Texas and Hawaii had been annexed with these "executive agreements" (agreements made between the president and the heads of foreign nations which do not receive the approval of two-thirds of the Senate). The "police action" in Korea had been both initiated and concluded by means of executive agreements; and at that very moment the United States' involvement in another

1

"police action"—in a small, unknown nation called Viet Nam (later respelled "Vietnam" by journalists who used the name so often that they wanted to make it easier to type)—was being slowly increased through a steady stream of executive agreements.

All of these actions were taken despite the fact that the term, and quite possibly the concept of, executive agreements was unknown to our Founding Fathers. Did the creators of our Constitution expect all foreign policy commitments to be concluded by treaty? How and why have executive agreements replaced treaties as the primary manner in which foreign policy compacts are concluded? Does the president now dominate the foreign policy arena so completely that executive power is unchecked?

The final question is really the crux of this study. If executive agreements are used solely to conclude routine matters such as postal agreements, which guarantee that each nation will deliver mail from other nations, then it does not really matter that the Senate is bypassed. However, if executive agreements are used to exclude Senate participation in the conclusion of important compacts, then the degree of presidential dominance in foreign policy becomes an issue.

This study must first demonstrate that presidents *do* conclude important matters with executive agreements in an attempt to avoid Senate interference. This will be done in two ways. A chapter covering the history of executive agreements will seek to outline cases where avoidance of the Senate was clearly a presidential goal. Second, all of the agreements and treaties ever made by the United States of America will be coded to differentiate between years when the Senate was dominated (two-thirds or more) by the party of the president, and years when this was not the case. An agreement-to-treaty ratio will be established for each year in an attempt to determine whether presidents have made many more agreements than treaties when their party was not in control of the Senate. If this has indeed been the case, then it would seem that presidents do use executive agreements to avoid the Senate.

If it becomes clear that executive agreements have been used successfully by presidents to avoid the Senate, then another question arises: What limitations exist to prevent presidents from using executive agreements to do whatever they wish in the foreign policy arena?

The potential barriers to unrestricted presidential control of foreign policy are the Senate's power of "advice and consent" with respect to treaties; Congress's control of the purse; and the federal courts, due to their self-appointed role as the interpreters of the Constitution. If the first barrier has been eliminated by the extensive usage of executive agreements, then the second two must be carefully evaluated.

The commoners in England used their control over the purse to wrest power gradually from the monarch and lords. Hence it comes as no surprise that our Founding Fathers decided that all requests for money would be initiated in the House of Representatives, the most democratic branch of government. (Some senators were elected by the state legislatures until 1913; and the president is selected by the electoral college, whose electors were also chosen by the state legislatures for the first few elections.)

Congresspeople and political scientists agree that the power of the purse is Congress's greatest power, for little can be done without money. Is this power still securely in the hands of Congress, or have presidents and other members of the executive branch found ways to obtain money without Congressional approval? If they have, then Congress's control over presidential foreign policy actions is far weaker than anyone has suspected, and the president's use of executive agreements is broader and more effective.

This use of funds for external affairs without specific Congressional approval will be an extremely difficult topic to research because of the desire of presidents to hide such activity from Congress. I have examined federal budgets, Congressional Research Office material, General Accounting Office reports, and the findings of other researchers to determine whether Congress controls the funding of external activities.

In the early case of *Marbury* v. *Madison*, the Supreme Court established itself as the primary interpreter of the Constitution. That decision made the Court a potential examiner of presidential actions in foreign policy as well, because affected parties could now challenge the constitutionality of executive agreements in the courts. In another chapter we shall look at the passages in the Constitution that are in any way related to executive agreements and at the Court's interpretation of these passages. The latter will be done through a review of the most important court cases that have involved executive agreements.

This work will seek to answer the questions that have been put forward in this introduction. It will also address a more important question: How much freedom *should* Congress give the president in the conduct of foreign affairs? Domination by one is efficient and secretive, but potentially tyrannical. Rule by a body (Congress) is safer, but the correct answer is vital if we are to conduct our foreign policy in the best manner possible.

NOTES

1. Alexander DeConde, ed., *Encyclopedia of American Foreign Policy* (New York: Charles Scribner's Sons, 1978), 339.

2. Arthur Schlesinger, Jr., *The Imperial Presidency* (Boston: Houghton Mifflin Company, 1973), 204.

2

A HISTORY
OF EXECUTIVE AGREEMENTS

The purpose of this chapter is twofold. A review of the role that executive agreements have played in the history of the United States will demonstrate their importance—thus justifying this study; it will also be shown that at least on a few occasions they have been used because presidents wished to avoid having to get a treaty through the Senate. In addition, this chapter will take note of the effects of changing environmental factors (technological advances, the United States' relations with neighbors, etc.) on the usage of executive agreements.

According to Wallace McClure in *International Executive Agreements*, the first executive agreement came when Timothy Pickering, postmaster general of the United States, offered the colonies of British North America (Canada) an exchange of postal services on March 17, 1792. However, Edward S. Corwin, writing in *The President's Control of Foreign Relations*, pp. 117-18, Arthur Schlesinger, Jr. in *The Imperial Presidency*, p. 86 and the *Treaties and Other International Agreements* series all concur that the first executive agreement was the Rush-Bagot agreement in 1817, in which the United States and Britain agreed to limit their naval forces on the Great Lakes.

The United States of America was in existence for over twenty-seven years before a president found it necessary to conclude an executive agreement; and this agreement, which demilitarized the Great Lakes, was clearly within the president's power as commander-in-chief. Why is it that in this day and age hundreds of executive agreements are concluded every year, including presidential commitments of U.S.

military support to nations such as Franco's Spain? What factors generated this change?

THE LOUISIANA PURCHASE

The Louisiana Purchase was, perhaps, a harbinger of this evolution. President Jefferson agreed to buy the Purchase from France, paid the agreed upon sum, and *then* submitted the proposition to the Senate for confirmation—implying that the deal had not been finalized (and also preventing historians and political scientists from labeling this action as executive agreement). What President Jefferson would have done with the land if the Senate had failed to provide the necessary two-thirds vote is only a matter for speculation. France had the money that she had requested, and it is almost inconceivable that she would have been willing to reverse the deal. In reality Louisiana had been purchased before the Senate even saw the terms that had been proposed.

It is ironic, to say the least, that Thomas Jefferson, the father of a political party whose primary aim had been to prevent the federal government from becoming too powerful (the Democratic-Republican Party), would take such a dramatic action before he had sought the "advice and consent" of the Senate. President Jefferson realized that his action did not reflect his words, or, indeed, his beliefs. The offer to buy all of Louisiana, rather than just New Orleans, arose unexpectedly. The price was just too good, and Napoleon was in too much of a hurry for Jefferson to hesitate. Jefferson was also in a hurry because he feared that Britain would conquer Louisiana before the Senate okayed the deal (or that Napoleon might even sell Louisiana to his enemy, Britain. The British would save lives, and Napoleon would have gotten something for the land.) British possession of Louisiana would have deprived the United States of invaluable land, and it also would have placed a hostile force at the southern border. The president's sense of propriety bowed before the urgency of the situation. Perhaps one of the reasons that so many more executive agreements are made in this day and age is that the United States faces so many more urgent situations.

The Louisiana Purchase, considered by most historians—but not by the author of this work—to be a treaty (remember, Jefferson did *pay* before the Senate even saw the terms), was an anomaly in early U.S. history. During this time period (1789-1860), executive agreements were used almost exclusively to resolve unimportant issues such as the settling of claims of individual U.S. citizens against foreign governments. Of the thirty-eight executive agreements made between 1789 and 1860, fourteen dealt with the settling of claims: four with Ecuador, and ten with Venezuela. It would seem that the presidents involved chose to avoid the treaty-making procedure in these cases because of their aforementioned insignificance and because no long-term commitments were involved. (This goes back to Vattel, who in *The Law of Nations* defined a "treaty," in Latin *foedus*, as "a compact made with a view to the public welfare, by the superior power, either for perpetuity or for a considerable time; whereas 'agreements,' 'conventions,' and 'pactions' have temporary matters for their object."[1] Vattel, who was considered to be one of the major legal scholars of that time, was an important influence upon both our Founding Fathers in their construction of the Constitution and our early presidents in their attempts to perform within its boundaries with respect to the questions of definition and usage of treaties and agreements.)

ANNEXATION OF TEXAS

The most significant early executive agreement was the one that brought about the annexation of Texas.

From the moment they began their insurrection in 1836, the Texans (mostly U.S. settlers who had sworn allegiance to Mexico) appealed to President Jackson either to recognize their independence or to annex them. Jackson wanted Texas, but he took no action because he feared both war with Mexico and the opposition of northern abolitionists. "After the Battle of San Jacinto (and victory), Texas asked to be annexed on terms calling for recognition of property in slaves. Abolitionists feared that Texas might become four or five slave states in the Union and argued that the Texas Revolution was part of a conspiracy by slave owners and those in power in the United States to gain more slave territory."[2]

Faced with such strong opposition, Jackson waited to recognize Texas as an independent nation (much less to annex it) until after Martin Van Buren, his hand-picked successor, had been elected to the presidency. (Jackson recognized Texas on March 3, 1837, his last full day in office.)

The Texan minister in Washington offered Texas for annexation to Van Buren, but he too refused out of fear of the Whigs and abolitionists. Therefore, Texas withdrew the offer of annexation, and took up the course of independence.

John Tyler was a proslavery Virginian. Previously a Democrat, he was given the second spot on the Whig ticket to bring Virginia over to William Henry Harrison. When President Harrison died soon after taking office, Tyler became president.

President Tyler wanted to bring Texas into the United States not only because it would be a slave state, but also because he feared that the English would come to dominate Texas.

In 1843 Mexico offered political autonomy and separate statehood if Texas would return to Mexican rule. Texas's president Sam Houston began negotiations with Mexico in order to put pressure on the United States.

Tyler had hoped to use the issue of annexation to help him win the presidential election of 1844; but he failed to receive the nomination of either major party. Tyler still hoped to bring Texas into the nation in order to strengthen the slave states; but when he submitted the treaty to the Senate, it was defeated by a large margin.

When James K. Polk, the Democratic nominee, was elected on an expansionist platform, it seemed that public opinion was in favor of expansion.

> Although sensitive to the shift of opinion in favor of annexation, Tyler knew that he could not obtain a two-thirds majority in the Senate to approve a treaty. When Congress assembled in December, therefore, he suggested annexation by joint resolution, which required only a simple majority of both houses. A resolution calling for annexation passed in the House of Representatives on January 25, 1845, by a vote of 120 to 98, and in the Senate on February 27, by 27 to 25.
>
> In both houses the vote followed party, rather than sectional, lines. All the Democrats voted in favor of the resolution, and all but two Whigs opposed it. Tyler signed it on March 1, three days before leaving office. Two days later he sent word to his diplomatic agent for Texas, Andrew J. Donelson, to invite Texas to join the Union under the terms of the resolution.
>
> Since the Constitution said "new states may be admitted by the Congress into this Union," the resolution invited Texas to come into the Union as a state, and not as a territory.[3]

The manner in which Texas was brought into the nation was quite significant in that it represented the first time that a president had made use of an executive agreement to avoid having to garner the two-thirds vote in the Senate that was required for a treaty. There was no precedent whatsoever for President Tyler's maneuver; but the realization that his political career was at an end may have inspired Tyler to attempt something that his successor, Polk, whose desire for reelection might engender a greater respect for the treaty process, would not dare. (President Tyler may have been inspired by a desire to aid the forces of slavery, or to improve his place in history, or any combination of the above. While the motive is interesting, it is the modus operandi that is important. For the first time an executive agreement was substituted for a treaty because of the recalcitrance of the Senate. A new, and some would argue a very dangerous, precedent had been set.)

The annexation of Texas did lead to war with Mexico, and the initial armistice was concluded by executive agreements in 1848. (The same thing occurred in the Spanish-American War [1898], although the final settlements of both wars consisted of treaties.)

EARLY AGREEMENTS WITH THE FAR EAST

In 1893 U.S. naval forces aided U.S. citizens living on Hawaii in removing Queen Liliuokalani from power. When President Cleveland learned of the interference by U.S. forces, he withdrew the treaty for annexation (which the new Hawaiian provisional government, consisting of U.S. sugar growers, had requested) from the Senate.

The expansionist Republicans began pushing for this treaty when William McKinley was elected to the presidency in 1896. However, anti-imperialist Democrats and Southerners from sugar-growing states blocked the treaty in the Senate. McKinley, facing the same problem as Tyler, chose the same solution. A joint resolution passed through both houses on July 6, 1898, and Hawaii was annexed as a territory by means of an executive agreement with the Hawaiian provisional government.

The United States' victory over Spain in the Spanish-American War (1898) left the United States with a large Asian dependency—the Philippines. The acquisition of so large a territory far from the United States had a definite impact on U.S. foreign policy. U.S. presidents became more aggressive and much more active in Asian affairs.

An example of the increased aggressiveness came when Santo Domingo faced bankruptcy and possible takeover by its European creditors in 1905. In order to save Santo Domingo, President Theodore Roosevelt sought Senate ratification of a treaty that would place Santo Domingo's customs houses under U.S. control. The Senate, however, declined ratification. Roosevelt, as he himself stated it, "put the agreement into effect, and I continued its execution for two years before the Senate acted; and I would have continued it until the end of my term, if necessary, without any action by Congress."[4]

The United States' increased interest in Asian affairs after the acquisition of the Philippines was demonstrated by an executive agreement with Japan in 1905. When the Russo-Japanese War began (1905), Korea had proclaimed independence. Japan, however, soon turned Korea into a protectorate.

> Japan's victories over Russia had caused some uneasiness in the United States over the safety of the Philippines. While on a trip to the Philippines, Secretary of War William Howard Taft, under Roosevelt's instructions, stopped off at Tokyo. In conversations there with Count Taro Katsura, Japan's prime minister, he brought up concern over the Philippines and also said that he believed Japanese suzerainty over Korea would contribute to lasting peace in the Far East. Katsura, in turn, disavowed any aggressive Japanese designs against the Philippines. Following this exchange of views, on July 27, 1905, an "agreed memorandum" of the discussion was drawn up, which some have called the "Taft-Katsura Agreement." Although the memorandum was not a formal agreement, it did embody the president's ideas. He cabled Taft that the conversation was absolutely correct and that "I confirm every word you have said."[5]

The year 1906 saw the beginning of a series of events that would lead to one of the least commendable agreements in U.S. history. On October 11, the San Francisco Board of Education passed a resolution that ordered the segregation of Chinese, Japanese, and Korean children. "Since the Chinese children were already under segregation, it was evident that the school order was aimed at the Japanese. It was alleged that the Japanese children were not only overcrowding the schools, but were vicious, immoral, and unfit to associate with white children."[6] Deeply insulted, the Japanese newspapers called for war. Perhaps motivated by altruism, but certainly concerned about the Philippines, President Theodore Roosevelt censured the Californians, and brought pressure upon them to yield. They, however, remained intransigent. The *San Francisco Chronicle* supported the contention that the Japanese were unassimilable and also argued that Japanese laborers, who were willing to work for lower wages, were lowering the U.S. standard of living.[7]

> On February 29 (1907) President Roosevelt signed an amendment to the Immigration Act of 1907, by virtue of which he was empowered to exclude from the United States immigrants holding passports to any country other than the United States, its insular possessions, or the Canal

Zone and attempting to use them to enter the United States. This successfully stemmed the flow of Japanese labor from Hawaii, Mexico, and Canada to the United States. As a *quid pro quo*, the San Francisco Board of Education on March 13 . . . rescinded the objectionable resolution insofar as it applied to the Japanese.[8]

Having successfuly ameliorated an uncomfortable situation, President Roosevelt now sought to eliminate the cause in a manner acceptable to the Japanese. A gentlemen's agreement was concluded: "By this agreement, the Japanese government pledged not to issue passports to laborers, skilled or unskilled, except to those who were domiciled in the United States, or to their families, namely parents, wives, and children."[9] The Japanese agreed to limit emigration, and U.S. immigration would take no further insulting action. This was the most palatable solution to a rather disgusting course of events. U.S. xenophobia had been prevented from completely alienating the most powerful nation in Asia.

Japan's importance in Asian affairs, and the United States' subsequent desire to bargain with, rather than to confront, that nation were apparent once again in the Root-Takahira agreement of 1908. An exchange of notes between Secretary of State Root and Ambassador Takahira indicated that the status quo in the region was acceptable to both sides—meaning that the Open Door Policy in China (all nations would have access to Chinese trade) and Chinese independence would remain intact, while the United States would allow Japan to retain its influence over Manchuria (a section of northeastern China).

The Lansing-Ishii agreement of 1917 sought to maintain this balance by reiterating the need for both the continued independence of China and the maintenance of the Open Door Policy, while recognizing that the "territorial propinquity" of Japan gave it "special interests" in China.

The United States' victory in the Spanish-American War not only established it as a world power but also made it a world power concerned more than ever before with the actions of others. The United States had acquired a piece of property, the Philippines, which had to be protected; and it had also acquired the taste for more property and more power. Wheeling and dealing with other world powers required both flexibility and secrecy. Hence executive agreements were used rather than treaties. After all, what might China have done upon learning from a U.S. Senate debate that the U.S. president sought a treaty with Japan that recognized Japanese influence over Manchuria or Japan's special interests in China? It is doubtful that China's door would have remained open to U.S. trade. Without the executive agreements being made with Japan, the United States would have had either to sacrifice trade with China (as Japan would have seized much, if not all, of China), or to have gone to war with Japan to prevent its conquest of China. Neither of these options was nearly as palatable to the United States as the secretive sacrifice of some of China's territorial integrity in exchange for keeping most of it, and hence trade with China, intact. The need for greater flexibility and secrecy that came with being a world power made the executive agreement a necessary tool more than ever before.

THE TWENTIETH CENTURY

The executive agreement not only increased the president's flexibility in dealing with other nations but also in dealing with his own Congress. An example of this is the debt owed to the United States by many European nations after World War I. The Europeans had expected the United States to cancel these debts, but Congress demanded payment in full, and Congress stated exactly this in a law passed in 1922. With the European nations unwilling to pay in full, and Congress unwilling to accept anything less, President Calvin Coolidge found himself caught in the middle. Established as the nation's leader in foreign policy by the Constitution, President Coolidge was rightfully concerned about angering all of the nations of Western Europe. The debt commission, therefore, negotiated thirteen executive agreements between 1923 and 1926, which were based upon the abilities of the European governments to pay.[10] Since the debt settlements did not adhere to the law passed in 1922, the commission had to seek congressional approval of each agreement. The fact that the debt commission had chosen to negotiate more lenient settlements rather than sticking to Congress's hard line, however, made it clear to Congress that the executive branch supported the requests of the Europeans. Hence Congress approved the agreements, and the executive agreement proved to be a useful tool for the president in dealing with his own legislature.

The United States' increasing role in world affairs mirrored her growing industrial might. As U.S. businesses became more and more active in foreign markets, the need for governmental protection increased. This led to an increased use of executive agreements. "In 1923 the United States and Mexico signed the Bucareli Agreement, which provided that confiscated land would be compensated for with Mexican bonds, and that Mexico would honor oil concessions if some positive development had taken place prior to the promulgation of the

1917 Constitution [which asserted public ownership of all Mexican petroleum rights]."[11] The Morrow-Calles Accord of 1928 settled a dispute over the U.S. oil companies' right to drill in Mexico. In this accord, Mexico confirmed the ownership of petroleum concessions held prior to 1917.

The increased use of executive agreements was not simply a product of presidents seeking to maximize their own power. Congresspeople realized that one individual—the president—could act with greater flexibility and speed than could a legislative body. Hence they were often willing to empower the president to use his discretion in carrying out the general will of Congress. In doing this, Congress yielded some of its power to the president.

An example of this phenomenon was the Reciprocal Trade Agreement amendment to the tariff act of 1930, which was passed in March of 1934.

> The Reciprocal Trade Agreements Act gave the president power, through bilateral executive agreements, to reduce existing tariff rates up to fifty per cent. It also embodied the unconditional form of the most-favored-nation principle. This principle meant that a trade concession to one country would automatically be extended to all other countries producing the same product, if they did not discriminate against American goods.
>
> Under the act, the administration could bargain with other governments for a reciprocal lowering of tariffs without the need of congressional approval for each agreement since Congress had given blanket consent beforehand. By making concessions on foreign imports, the government could persuade other countries to reduce their duties on American goods. . . . From the time the Reciprocal Trade Act was passed to January 1940, the United States signed agreements with twenty-one countries which accounted for sixty per cent of American foreign trade.[12]

For the most part executive agreements have been used to perform routine functions either explicitly or implicitly acceptable to Congress. However, one should not underestimate the ability of presidents to use executive agreements to alter U.S. foreign policy in the face of a neutral, or even hostile, Congress. U.S. involvement in World War II and "that crazy Asian war" (Vietnam) was brought about by means of these agreements.

Before the Japanese attack on Pearl Harbor (which brought the United States into the war), most U.S. citizens wanted to avoid becoming embroiled in World War II because they saw it as a European war for colonies. Even while the war progressed badly for Great Britain, the United States' closest post-World War I ally, most of the U.S. public still favored neutrality.

Losses of destroyers to German submarines and the Luftwaffe (the German air force) had put the British navy in a bad way. Destroyers were needed to protect vital sea lanes and to patrol the coastline. Even though the United States was a neutral nation, President Franklin D. Roosevelt gave Britain fifty over-age destroyers that had been tied up in U.S. ports. In return, the United States received leases to Caribbean bases on British possessions ranging from the Bahamas to Guyana.

> Roosevelt's deed made the United States a virtual ally of Britain, violated existing international law, and may have violated domestic law forbidding the sale of military property to a foreign government. The attorney general justified the act on the principle of retaliation. Hitler's aggressions and repeated flouting of international law, he said, released the United States from the rules of neutrality.[13]

In March 1941, FDR transferred ten Coast Guard cutters to the British to aid them in antisubmarine operations.

On April 10, 1941, the State Department announced an agreement with the Danish minister in Washington (promptly disavowed by the captive government in Copenhagen) which gave the United States the right to occupy Greenland during the emergency (while Germany occupied Denmark) for defense purposes.

On August 9, 1941, Roosevelt met with Winston Churchill aboard the cruiser *Augusta*. They arranged for the U.S. navy to escort British as well as U.S. ships in the convoys of the North Atlantic.[14]

In September 1941, FDR advanced the Soviets $100 million in credit to be repaid in the indefinite future with shipments of manganese, platinum, and other raw materials.

Later in September, special U.S. and British missions went to Moscow to appraise Soviet needs. The U.S. promptly promised the Soviets approximately $1 billion worth of supplies, including tanks, planes, and guns. In October FDR declared the Soviet Union eligible for lend-lease aid.[15]

It is not for me to judge whether these actions were "wise"; but they certainly were not the actions of a supposedly neutral nation. Without consulting Congress, a president had succeeded in changing the status of the United States from neutral to belligerent.

> At the White House on New Year's Day, 1942, Roosevelt and Churchill, Ambassador Maxim Litvinov for the Soviet Union, and representatives of twenty-three other nations at war with Axis powers, brought the grand

coalition into existence by signing the Declaration of the United Nations. It bound signatory governments to an alliance against the Axis, to uphold the Atlantic Charter, and not to make a separate peace. With this executive agreement, never submitted to the Senate, Roosevelt defied the tradition of nonentanglement.[16]

World War II greatly altered the balance of power in the world. The prewar powers—Britain, France, and Germany—were all greatly weakened; and two new nations—the United States and the Soviet Union—suddenly held the balance of power. Franklin D. Roosevelt was quick to assume the mantle of leadership.

In July of 1944 the administration sponsored the United Nations Monetary and Financial Conference at Bretton Woods, a resort in the mountains of New Hampshire. The Bretton Woods Conference sought to prevent "a return to the monetary chaos of the 1930's—the unstable exchanges and the competitive depreciations, the exchange controls and the inconvertible currencies of that era of economic warfare."[17]

The nations decided to return to a modified version of the gold-exchange standard of the 1920s, and "to back up the revived standard the Bretton Woods Conference created the International Monetary Fund, a complex endowment of gold and national currencies designed to help deficit countries to finance temporary imbalances of payments. It was hoped that the Fund would ensure relatively stable exchanges, an early return to convertibility, and, in general, international monetary cooperation."[18]

As the end of World War II drew near, President Roosevelt met with Stalin and Churchill at Yalta.

Stalin made concessions on German reparations, on voting arrangements in the projected world organization, on the question of a French zone of occupation in Germany, and on several other matters. Moreover, the date of Russia's entrance into the war against Japan was fixed. Yet Stalin also gained some large demands. While the conference did not "give" him Poland, which was already occupied by Red troops, the terms of the agreement may have facilitated ensuing Soviet control of that country. And in the Far East Stalin was granted the Kurile Islands, the southern part of Sakhalin, and extensive spheres of influence in North China.[19]

After the death of President Roosevelt, the new president, Harry Truman, met with Stalin and Churchill at Potsdam. In a "package" deal the Soviets agreed to the admission of Italy into the United Nations after a peace treaty was arranged; the United States and Great Britain agreed to set the temporary western border of Poland at the

Oder-Neisse line; and the Soviets settled for far less in reparations than they had expected.[20]

The agreements made at Yalta and Potsdam were of profound importance. They not only altered the spheres of influence of the major powers, but they may also have been the stepping stones that led the United States and the Soviet Union into an era of confrontation that would be known as the "Cold War." However, *all* of these agreements were made by presidents without the advice and consent of the Senate.

The end of the Second World War signaled not only a new balance of power, with the United States and the USSR leading their respective blocs, but also a new type of power: atomic energy. The Western bloc looked to the United States for protection because it alone possessed this power. As the Soviets made technological advances in atomic energy, long-range bombers, and guided missiles, the United States looked to its allies not only for military support but also locations for radar stations. For example, the previously mentioned Soviet technological gains gave the Arctic regions of Canada a strategic importance they had not previously held.

> At the urging of the United States, Canadian officials early in 1947 discussed plans for defense of the northland. One result was the declaration on defense announced on February 12 from Washington and Ottawa. The two English-speaking countries agreed to collaborate "for peacetime joint security purposes" by continuing indefinitely the Permanent Joint Board on Defense of 1941. This cooperation included standardization of arms and equipment as well as reciprocal use of military, naval, and air facilities in each country. Since the agreement rested on no contractual obligation, each country could at any time end the collaboration.[21]

In 1950 the United States and Canada began work on a joint radar network, the "Pinetree Chain," stretching across Canada just north of the U.S. border. "A year later, on March 27, they signed a civil defense mutual aid agreement, envisaging coordination in civil defense activities in time of war 'as if there were no border.' In October 1953 they carried their cooperation a step further by agreeing on a second joint radar network some five hundred miles north of the Pinetree Chain, called the 'Mid-Canada Line.'"[22] In May of 1955 an executive agreement was made for the construction of a third radar warning line near Canada's northern limits called the Distant Early Warning System, the DEW line, for short.

In her new position as the leader of the Western world, the United States sought to strengthen alliances by creating numerous treaty organizations: the North Atlantic Treaty Organization (NATO), the Southeast Asian Treaty Organization (SEATO), ANZUS (with Australia and New Zealand), and so forth. Numerous executive agreements were made in order to further these alliances—agreements offering things such as military and technical know-how, loans of naval vessels and money, and so on.

Francisco Franco's friendship with Adolf Hitler and the repressive practices of his regime caused Spain to be excluded from NATO. Spain's location, however, made it vital to the defense of Western Europe. Hence the United States sought rapprochement with Spain beginning in 1950,

> when Congress authorized extension of $62.5 million in loans to Spain and President Truman announced that he was appointing an ambassador to fill the Madrid post that had been vacant since 1945. Finally, in September 1953, the United States signed three agreements with Spain, known collectively as the Pact of Madrid, that made available $226 million in economic and military aid, already appropriated by Congress. In return, the Spaniards allowed the United States to build and use naval and air bases in their country. Those bases were completed in 1958, and indirectly Spain became a part of Western Europe's military system.[23]

(President Kennedy's declaration of mutual protection in 1963, discussed in the introduction, extended the U.S. umbrella of protection to Spain.)

While some of the postwar treaty organizations (SEATO, Central Treaty Organization or CENTO) have grown weak, or even have disintegrated, NATO is too vital to the security of its members for this to be allowed to occur. Thus it was that John F. Kennedy came to the presidency determined to reinvigorate U.S. efforts to promote European unity and Atlantic partnership. In 1962 he persuaded Congress to pass the Trade Expansion Act, which gave the president sweeping new powers (for five years) to negotiate reductions in tariffs by as much as fifty percent.[24] It was hoped that liberalized Atlantic trade would bring the U.S. and Western Europe closer together.

The Cuban missile crisis in October of 1962 led to an agreement between Kennedy and Nikita Khrushchev to install an emergency phone and teletype, or "hot line," connection between Washington and Moscow in June 1963. It was hoped that improved communication between the two superpowers might improve relations and, at least, lessen the chances of a nuclear war breaking out by accident.

The most recent series of executive agreements involved the Camp David accords. President Jimmy Carter promised economic and military aid to both Israel and Egypt in exchange for their agreement to make peace.

VIETNAM

The classic example of what a president can achieve with executive agreements is the gradual deepening of U.S. involvement in Vietnam.

This involvement began in February 1950, when, despite the claims of Ho Chi Minh, "the U.S. accorded diplomatic recognition to the Governments of the State of Vietnam, the Kingdom of Laos, and the Kingdom of Cambodia as independent states within the French Union."[2 5] (Ho Chi Minh had been the leader of the Vietnamese resistance forces who battled the Japanese after they replaced French control of Vietnam with their own. Even though the United States sought self-determination for most prewar colonies, Ho Chi Minh's admitted Marxist leanings caused the United States to agree to a return of French control in supposedly diluted form.)

Within a few months of according recognition, the United States decided to provide economic aid directly to Cambodia, Laos, and Vietnam, instead of channeling this aid through NATO as had been done before. The United States agreed that France should have a role in coordinating aid programs to these nations. "In August 1950 a Military Assistance Advisory Group of thirty-five men was sent to Indochina to advise on the use of American equipment."[2 6] In 1953 the United States loaned the French forces in Vietnam six C-119 transport planes. The United States also provided CIA-controlled Civil Air Transport service pilots to fly them.

The supplementary aid agreement on Indochina between the United States and France consisted of six letters exchanged between the U.S. ambassador to France, Douglas Dillon, and French Foreign Minister Georges Bidault on September 29, 1953. The United States promised to provide an additional $385 million beyond the aid already promised before 1955.

Although Cambodia, Laos, and Vietnam were not members of SEATO, the provisions of the SEATO treaty were applied to them by a special protocol on September 8, 1954, the day that SEATO was formed. In addition, the eight members of SEATO proclaimed the Pacific Charter, an executive agreement "upholding the principles of equal rights and self-determination and promising to strive to promote self-government and to secure the independence of all peoples that desire it and are able to undertake its responsibilities."[2][7]

"On October 24, 1961, President Kennedy sent a letter to President Ngo Dinh Diem saying: 'Let me assure you again that the United States is determined to help Viet-Nam preserve its independence, protect its people against Communist assassins and build a better life through economic growth.'"[2][8] Four months later President Kennedy sent 300 more men to Saigon, bringing the number of U.S. personnel in Vietnam to 4,000. In 1961 Kennedy "authorized Ambassador Nolting, U.S. Ambassador to South Vietnam, to tell Diem that the United States would step up military and economic aid, increase its advisors, and collaborate with Saigon in the direction of the war effort, in return for implementation of the political and administrative reforms discussed late in 1960 and early 1961."[2][9] JFK offered aircraft, training, and economic aid if Diem would seek to broaden popular support for his government, seek to mobilize all his nation's resources, and overhaul the command structure so as to create a more effective military organization. Diem's refusal to comply with these demands caused the United States to support—if not engineer—his removal.

In 1962 the United States signed the Geneva Agreement on Laos, along with the two Vietnams, Communist China, the USSR, and numerous other nations. This agreement proclaimed the neutrality of Laos.

In August of 1964, President Johnson, claiming that two U.S. destroyers had been attacked in international waters by North Vietnamese torpedo boats, asked for and received congressional support in the form of the Gulf of Tonkin Resolution "for all necessary action to protect our armed forces and to assist nations covered by the SEATO Treaty." Even before this, however, was not the United States verbally committed to South Vietnam? Executive agreements gave Vietnam the protection that the United States guaranteed to SEATO members; and verbal commitments seemed to make it clear that the United States was determined to do whatever was necessary to preserve the territorial integrity of South Vietnam. Without consulting Congress, Presidents Truman, Eisenhower, and Kennedy had slowly but steadily committed the United States to a course of action.

It seems only fitting that executive agreements, which played such a large role in getting the United States into Vietnam, helped in getting her out. In October 1972, Henry Kissinger and Le Duc Tho of North Vietnam worked out a truce agreement:

Hanoi agreed to a cease-fire twenty-four hours after the signing of an accord. The United States promised to stop all "acts of war" against North Vietnam at the same time. Americans would within sixty days withdraw troops from South Vietnam, both sides would release military prisoners, and various South Vietnamese political groups would participate in general elections. The agreement forbade both the United States and North Vietnam to send fresh armaments into the South, but permitted North Vietnamese troops, estimated at 145,000 to remain there.[30]

While this agreement did not hold, and the bombing of North Vietnam was resumed, these same conditions made up the truce agreement signed on January 27, 1973. President Nixon promised President Nguyen Van Thieu of South Vietnam that if his nation went along with the Paris peace agreement, then the United States would continue to provide aid. In addition, Nixon promised that "we will respond with full force should the settlement be violated by North Vietnam."[31]

Nixon and Kissinger promised North Vietnam a "preliminary" figure of $3.25 billion in grant aid over a period of five years, with other forms of aid to be negotiated if North Vietnam agreed to the Paris peace agreement. However, because North Vietnam refused to ensure a ceasefire in Cambodia, the United States finally refused to complete an agreement for postwar assistance. (It would have been interesting to see if Congress would have been willing to fund such an arrangement.)

These illustrations demonstrate both the versatility of executive agreements and some of the reasons why their use has increased so greatly. The versatility can be seen in the fact that they have been used both to perform routine tasks such as settling the claims of individual U.S. citizens—something far too insignificant for the Senate to be bothered with ratifying—and to commit the United States to support the governments of Franco's Spain and South Vietnam, to name some controversial cases, to a degree which the Senate might not have approved.

The evolution of executive agreements is more difficult to understand in that it is hard to differentiate between the changes that were caused by the events of the time (the political situation, etc.) and those that came about because of the individual characteristics of certain presidents. Thomas Jefferson's purchase of the Louisiana Territory (which I consider to be the first executive agreement) was executed without first being submitted to the Senate because the situation demanded it. The territory was too vital to U.S. interests, and Napoleon was in too big a hurry to find a buyer, for Jefferson to wait for the senators to complete a thorough examination. John Tyler's motives for annexing Texas without going through the treaty process are more difficult to fathom. Tyler's three predecessors, Andrew Jackson, Martin Van Buren, and William Henry Harrison had had the option to attempt to annex Texas, but they had not even tried. (Harrison, the only Whig of the three, opposed the annexation, but Jackson and Van Buren were both Democrats, and they did want to bring Texas into the United States.) Tyler's willingness to use an executive agreement when the Senate refused to provide the two-thirds majority for the proposed treaty, an action considered quite extreme in that day, sprang from bitterness, anger, and a desire to accomplish a remarkable feat before leaving office. John Tyler had become president upon William Henry Harrison's death. Even though he was eligible for reelection, neither party nominated him to head its ticket. Thus it was that Tyler was driven to do something that his beloved South would remember him for—the annexation of Texas. Besides annexing Texas, Tyler also established the precedent of presidents using executive agreements when the Senate was adamant.

The United States' coming of age as a world power in the latter part of the nineteenth century furthered U.S. presidents' usage of executive agreements. For the first time the United States had a large overseas possession, the Philippines, and the need to protect it. This lessened the United States' isolation from the rest of the world, and it also seemed to whet the United States' appetite for more property and more power. The colonial powers of Western Europe often made secret agreements with one another (for example, Britain, France, Russia, and nine other nations, including the United States, all yielded parts of China to one another in exchange for the recognition of their respective claims). Executive agreements became more necessary because of the need for secrecy. U.S. presidents did not want potential adversaries both at home—many citizens opposed any type of colonialism—and abroad to know what was being done.

The United States emerged from World War II as one of two major powers. The invention of nuclear weapons and long-range bombers and missiles made a return to isolationism impractical if not impossible. These factors put an even greater premium on secrecy and speed as well. Thus it was that U.S. presidents began making many more executive agreements after World War II than they ever had before, as will be discussed in detail in this work.

As the world changed, and as the United States' role in the world changed, executive agreements became more and more a part of U.S. foreign policy. While this chapter has been focused on the most significant, and often the most controversial, agreements in U.S. history, it remains to be seen just how representative these are of executive agreements as a whole. Have executive agreements become so prominent because of the greater number of interactions with other nations, because of the greater need for speed and secrecy, because of an increased desire by presidents to avoid the Senate, or rather because of some combination of these? Do the benefits of their use outweigh the drawbacks?

NOTES

1. James F. Barnett, "International Agreements without the Advice and Consent of the Senate," *Yale Law Journal* 15 (1905-1906):20.

2. Alexander DeConde, *A History of American Foreign Policy* (New York: Charles Scribner's Sons, 1978), 1:170.

3. Ibid., 1:174.

4. Arthur Schlesinger, Jr., *The Imperial Presidency* (Boston: Houghton Mifflin Company, 1973), pp. 87-88.

5. DeConde, *A History of American Foreign Policy*, 1:335.

6. Chitoshi Yanaga, *Japan Since Perry* (New York: McGraw-Hill Book Company, 1949), p. 434.

7. Ibid., pp. 436-437.

8. Ibid., p. 437.

9. Ibid., p. 438.

10. DeConde, *A History of American Foreign Policy*, 1:131-132.

11. Stephen D. Krasner, *Defending the National Interest* (Princeton, N.J.: Princeton University Press, 1978), p. 161.

12. DeConde, *A History of American Foreign Policy*, 2:138.

13. Ibid., 2:157.

14. Ibid., 2:164.

15. Ibid., 2:166.

16. Ibid., 2:174-176.

17. *American Foreign Economic Policy*, ed. Benjamin J. Cohen (New York: Harper and Row, Publishers, 1968), p. 37.

18. Ibid., p. 37.

19. James MacGregor Burns, *Roosevelt: The Lion and the Fox* (New York: Harcourt, Brace, and World, Inc., 1956), p. 469.

20. Barton J. Bernstein, ed. and intro., *Politics and Policies of the Truman Administration* (Chicago: Quadrangle Books, 1970), p. 30.

21. DeConde, *A History of American Foreign Policy*, 2:261.

22. Ibid., 2:261-262.

23. Ibid., 2:310.

24. Cohen, ed., *American Foreign Economic Policy*, p. 187.

25. Amy M. Gilbert, *Executive Agreements and Treaties, 1946-1973* (Endicott, N.Y.: Thomas-Newell, 1973), p. 37.

26. Ibid., p. 38.

27. Ibid., p. 41.

28. Ibid., p. 83.

29. Gareth Porter, ed., Vietnam: *The Definitive Documentation of Human Decisions*, 2 vols. (Stanfordville, N.Y.: Earl M. Coleman Enterprises, Inc., Publishers, 1979), 2:146.

30. DeConde, *A History of American Foreign Policy*, 2:377.

31. Porter, ed., *Vietnam: The Definitive Documentation of Human Decisions*, 2:592.

3

PROBLEMS IN STUDYING
EXECUTIVE AGREEMENTS
AND METHODOLOGY

THE PROBLEMS

The relative scarcity of works dealing specifically with executive agreements would seem to indicate that executive agreements either are not considered to be worth studying or are simply too difficult to study in depth. In the chapter dealing with the history of executive agreements, it became apparent that executive agreements have been and remain an often used and vital tool of the president in foreign policy. We now address the complexities and methodology of studying these agreements.

The main problems that arise in studying executive agreements are those of definition and secrecy. The traditional problem of definition with respect to executive agreements deals with the term itself. Just what exactly is an "executive agreement"?

Elmer Plischke defined an executive agreement as "an understanding with another country entered into by the president of the United States without the consent of the Senate, which would be required to approve a treaty. It's principal distinction from a treaty is less a matter of substance than of intent and process."[1]

Louis Fisher stated that "The primary boundary between treaties and executive agreements has never been defined to anyone's satisfaction. Of course treaties require the advice and consent of the Senate, while executive agreements do not. As a second distinction, treaties (unlike executive agreements) may supercede prior conflicting statutes."[2] (The chapter that deals with court cases will show that Mr. Fisher's second distinction is not correct for all cases.)

There is substantial consensus that an executive agreement is an agreement made by the president, or by a presidentially authorized individual, with the head (or an authorized representative) of a foreign country, which has not been approved by the Senate before it goes into effect. However, there is another problem of definition which must be dealt with: At what point does an executive agreement (oral or written) become an executive agreement? If the president promises the head of a foreign nation something, but then has a change of mind, has an agreement been made and then terminated, or never made at all? What if the president promises the head of a foreign nation something but is then unable to deliver? Does this constitute an executive agreement? In my opinion, both of these actions constitute executive agreements; but the problems described in these cases have nothing to do with what were coded as executive agreements in this study.

As my sample, I utilized all of the agreements and treaties that appeared in the *Treaties and Other International Agreements of the United States of America* series.[3] According to an act of Congress on July 8, 1966, the TIA series is now "competent evidence of the treaties, international agreements other than treaties . . . in all the courts of law . . . and public offices of the United States . . . without any further proof or authentication thereof."[4] However, this series only includes agreements that appeared at one time or another on paper. Agreements that remained oral are not accounted for in the TIA series, or subsequently, in my chapter dealing with an analysis of executive agreements and treaties in a mathematical manner. (The chapter dealing with the history of executive agreements does include some oral agreements as described by other authors.)

The second problem is the one of secrecy. For both military and political reasons, national leaders often seek to conceal their actions from their domestic and foreign opponents. Students of the U.S. presidency have long been confronted by this problem and often stymied by it. Neither I nor anyone else can be sure of just what portion of all executive agreements we actually have knowledge. Even the presidents who engineered such agreements can only be sure of those made during their administration. However, it is my opinion that the diligent actions of a free press, probing by political scientists and historians, and the willingness of most presidents to submit to the people's need to know in a democracy have made all but a very small percentage of executive agreements common knowledge.

Another problem is whether all agreements are equally significant, or whether "more important" ones should be weighed more heavily. To offer the most representative presentation, I have chosen to use two methods of analysis. One counts all agreements equally, while the other divides them into types.

TYPES OF AGREEMENTS

It is an understatement to say that an executive agreement which provides for mutual postal delivery by two nations' postal services differs greatly from one that provides for each to come to the defense of the other in the case of an attack. In an attempt to gain a better understanding of the topics to be analyzed, I have divided executive agreements and treaties into three categories: (1) those which deal with procedural matters, and tend to be made as a matter of routine; (2) those which deliver material goods; and (3) those which deal with the military.

Postal agreements, reciprocal trade agreements, agreements providing for extradition, and civil aviation agreements are examples of the first type of agreements, which set the rules and regulations that make it easier for nations to live together. These agreements are usually made as a matter of routine with a large number of nations.

The second type of agreements involves those that provide a concrete good such as agricultural aid, technical assistance, and relief.

The third type, defense-related agreements, involves such things as mutual defense assistance, the loan of naval vessels, and the sending of military missions.

These categories were not chosen arbitrarily. The primary goal was to separate those agreements that are made as a matter of routine, and hence not greatly influenced by who the president is, from those in which the president takes a more active role. The procedural agreements (such as postal agreements) are usually engineered by bureaucrats without a large degree of presidential oversight. Defense-related agreements usually involve the Department of Defense and the State Department, and, of course, the president. Agreements which promise concrete goods are usually put into effect by the State Department in conjunction with at least one other bureaucratic agency, and the president. Hence we see that not only does the content of these types of agreements differ but so do the actors involved.

Whenever an attempt is made to place individual entities into broad categories, a degree of distortion is unavoidable. An example of this is the decision to place reciprocal trade agreements in the first category (procedural). The decision to lower tariffs between nations does involve a very concrete good—money. However, since it is a benefit to all the nations involved (instead of a grant of some sort from one to the other), and since the gain or loss is only potential (no trade, no gain), I chose to place this type of agreement in the first category. While my choice of categories does have some problems, I feel that it does increase our understanding of the topic at hand.

SPECIFIC PROBLEMS THAT AROSE IN THIS STUDY

When treaties are negotiated, there is often a lag between the time when they are concluded and the time when they go into effect. In this study, treaties of this type will be "credited" to the president during whose administration they were signed.

A more difficult problem arises when a treaty's negotiation begins during the term of one president, but is concluded during the term of another. Since treaties are used in this study to measure presidential activity, I have chosen to credit the president who initiated the treaty negotiations, not the president who concluded the treaty. The initiator of the negotiations usually does more to bring about the treaty's passage than does the president under whose administration the treaty is finally concluded. Furthermore, this type of treaty is very rare, so this system should not have much influence on my findings. Executive agreements almost always go into effect either immediately, or very soon after negotiations are concluded. Therefore, the aforementioned problems rarely arise in the case of executive agreements.

THE UNIT OF MEASUREMENT

In this section, executive agreements and treaties will be used to test certain theories about presidential activity and actions. The unit of time used will be the "presidential year," which is a period of 365 days beginning on the day when a president takes office. (Presidents assumed their positions on March 4 before 1940, and on January 20 beginning in 1940. Hence "presidential years" go from March 4-March 4 before 1940, and from January 20-January 20 from 1940 onward.) In the cases where an odd occurrence caused a president to take office on a day other than the normal one, I have chosen to readjust mathematically that time period to a full year for certain measurements. (For example, a president who came into office on December 20, one month before the normal time, and made ten agreements, would be credited with 120 [10 × 12 months/year] for his first "presidential year." Such adjustments will be indicated in the individual charts.) Because so few agreements were made before 1933, statistically significant findings are often impossible to calculate. Therefore most charts only deal with the period from 1933 to 1979.

CONTROLLING FOR OTHER FACTORS

When trying to measure a given phenomenon, it is essential that as many other influential factors be controlled for as is possible. Put more simply: in order to measure the influence of *one* factor, we must find a way to eliminate the influence of other factors on our measurement. An example of this would be an attempt to measure the influence of gender on the propensity to vote in local elections. Say that our figures showed that a higher percentage of men vote than of women. Does this indicate that gender is an important influence on who will vote? It might, but it also might not. Let's say that another look at our figures indicated that individuals with a college education voted at a higher rate than individuals with only a high school education. In order to control for the influence of education on our measure of the influence of gender, we would look to see if women with a college education voted at an equal rate as men with the same degree of education. If they did in this and the other categories, then we might learn that women as a group voted less than men as a group because the women were not as educated as the men—not because they were women. Had we not controlled for the influence of education, we would have come to an erroneous conclusion about the influence of gender on the propensity to vote.

In an attempt to learn whether presidents make executive agreements to avoid the Senate, I shall seek to control for such other variables as the influence of time, political party, state of war, newness of the job, taking office after a tragedy, the target nation, elections, and the individual presidents themselves. I shall utilize both the *number* of executive agreements (including treaties in some measures), and the *types* of executive agreements made.

NOTES

1. Elmer Plischke, in the *Encyclopedia Americana* (International Edition) (Danbury, Conn.: Grolier, 1981), 10:759.

2. Louis Fisher, *The Constitution Between Friends* (New York: St. Martin's Press, 1978), p. 204.

3. U.S., Department of State, *Treaties and Other International Agreements Series*.

4. Amy Gilbert, *Executive Agreements and Treaties, 1946-1973* (Endicott, N.Y.: Thomas-Newell, 1973), p. 8.

4

DO PRESIDENTS USE
EXECUTIVE AGREEMENTS
TO AVOID THE SENATE?

The purpose of this chapter is to determine whether presidents use executive agreements to avoid the Senate and the two-thirds vote needed for the passage of a treaty. In order to measure this accurately, a wide range of factors will be tested for their influence on the making of executive agreements, and those which are influential will be controlled for when the factor of avoiding the Senate is to be measured.

TIME

It is a time honored maxim in political science that the world has "grown smaller" over time as communications and transportation have been improved. The improvements in transportation have also improved the ability of nations to make war on those who are far away—which has made the world seem much, much smaller. This maxim would seem to dictate that there should be a steady increase in the number of agreements and treaties made between nations over time. Table 2 (all tables appear in Appendix A) seems to indicate that this is true. In the years 1789-1800 the United States made less than one agreement and treaty (combined) per year, rising to approximately one agreement and three treaties per year from 1800-1900. From 1900 to 1933, approximately twelve agreements and twelve treaties were the yearly averages. The "modern" era of U.S. politics, 1933-79, saw the average number of agreements made per year jump to nearly 183, while the yearly average of treaties remained at twelve. In addition, Table 4 indicates that the most agreements and treaties ever made were during the administrations of Presidents Ford and Carter —the most recent administrations considered. However, Table 4 also indicates that there has not been a steady increase in the number of treaties and agreements made over time. President Truman, who was in office from 1945 to 1953, made almost as many agreements and treaties as did President Johnson, who served from 1963 to 1969. President Eisenhower (1953-61) made more agreements and treaties per year than did President Nixon (1969-74).

What about the types of treaties and agreements that were made? Tables 1B, 2B, and 3B indicate that there have not been any clear themes running through the years from Franklin Roosevelt through Richard Nixon. The number of defense-related agreements (labeled "military" in the tables) increased in the later years of the Truman administration and peaked during the Eisenhower years (at 48.9 per year). There was a decline in the Kennedy years, followed by a sharp decline during the Johnson administration (18.8 per year). The level of activity with respect to military-related agreements remained at roughly half the yearly number of the Eisenhower years through the first two years of Jimmy Carter.

The average yearly number of agreements that provided concrete goods was virtually the same in the Nixon years as it was during the Truman administration.

The number of procedural agreements remained fairly constant from Truman through Eisenhower, only to undergo a gradual increase starting with John Kennedy's administration and continuing through the Nixon years. This increase, however, was sporadic, not steady.

EXPLAINING THE JUMP

Table 1 indicates that foreign policy activity increased greatly during World War II and continued to increase after World War II. Around 1948 President Truman reached a level of activity (236 agreements and treaties concluded) which was comparable to that of any of his successors up to President Ford (see Figure 1). This would seem to indicate that the best explanation for the increase in U.S. foreign policy activity is historical. The second world war made the United States both willing and able to be more active in world affairs; and the destruction that the war wrought upon the prewar major powers left the United States as one of only two superpowers and the leader of the Western bloc. The United States was willing to accept these roles, and they led to a number of foreign policy commitments.

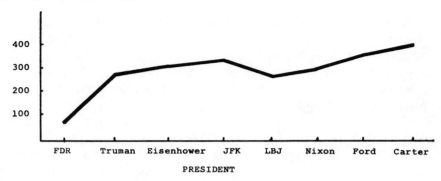

Figure 1. Average Number of Agreements and Treaties Made per Year by Each Modern President

What is interesting is that the number of these commitments seemed to remain relatively constant from the days of Truman through the days of Nixon.

The jump in the number of agreements and treaties made per year that began while Ford was president and continued through the two years of the Carter presidency that were studied is not as easy to explain. In Ford's first full year as president, he made 291 executive agreements. This leaped to 363 in the next, and final, year of his presidency. Jimmy Carter kept up this rapid rate by making 371 executive agreements during his first year in office, followed by a drop down to 299 in his second year. Still, while President Johnson averaged 205.6 agreements per year, and President Nixon averaged 223, Presidents Ford and Carter averaged 298 and 335 agreements per year, respectively.

A comparison of Nixon's and Ford's agreements reveals that in the Ford years there was a 30.7 percent increase in the number of routine agreements (procedural), a 50.2 percent increase in agreements providing concrete goods, and a 9.7 decrease in defense-related (military) agreements.

A comparison of Ford's and Carter's agreements reveals that in the Carter years there was a 1.2 percent increase in the number of procedural agreements, a 28 percent increase in the number of agreements providing concrete goods, and a 32.4 percent decrease in defense-related agreements.

Hence the findings indicate that most of the increase came from agreements providing goods, and a substantial portion came from procedural agreements, while the number of defense-related agreements declined. Unfortunately, I cannot explain the reason for the sudden increase in the numbers of these types of agreements.

ELECTIONS

One factor that may need to be controlled for is elections. Running for reelection takes a great deal of time. Candidates for the presidency often begin running a full year before the election takes place. What is the effect, if any, of having an incumbent president running for reelection upon U.S. foreign policy?

Hypothesis: Presidents who are eligible for reelection will make fewer agreements and treaties during the fourth year of their term than they averaged in the previous three years.

Alternative
Hypothesis: Presidents who are eligible for reelection will make more agreements and treaties during the fourth year of their term than they averaged in the previous three years.

The best explanation for the first hypothesis, should it be the case, is that incumbent presidents spend so much of their time trying to get reelected that they neglect foreign policy concerns. In these circumstances we would expect most of this decrease to be in agreements that provide concrete goods and those related to defense. This would be the case because procedural agreements are, for the most part, made as a matter of routine by the bureaucracy, whereas the other two types of agreements are a much better reflection of presidential desires and activity. The decrease in activity would reflect a preoccupation with reelection on the part of the president.

The best explanation for the alternative hypothesis, should it prove to be true, is that incumbent presidents, seeking to impress the voters with their accomplishments as the election nears, find it much easier to get things done in the foreign policy arena than in the domestic. This is the case because first, the Constitution set the presidency up as the main force in foreign affairs by including in the position the responsibilities of commander-in-chief, negotiator of treaties, and receiver of ambassadors; and second, congresspeople tend to be more concerned about domestic policy than foreign, because through the years domestic policy has a more direct effect upon their constituents, or at least their constituents believe this to be the case, so congresspeople allow the president more leeway in foreign affairs. For these reasons, we would expect the increase to be primarily in agreements that provide concrete goods and those related to defense.

Table 1 indicates that there may be some validity to hypothesis 2. In four of the eight cases considered (where the president served the four years and was eligible for reelection, with the exception of Truman's first term, when he served all but three months of FDR's last term), the greatest number of agreements and treaties was made in the fourth year. In the case of Truman's second term, the number of agreements and treaties made in the fourth year was only 2.7 percent greater than the total for the next highest year. The other three cases demonstrated much greater differentiation, with differences of 16.1 percent, 25 percent, and 37.8 percent.

Table 6 also shows that hypothesis 2 might have some validity. In six of the eight cases, the number of agreements and treaties made in the fourth year was greater than the average number of treaties and agreements made per annum in the first three years. However, when we control for the fact that presidents tend to make fewer agreements in their first year, we see that the number of agreements made in the fourth year was greater than the average for the second and third years in only four of eight cases. (This phenomenon will be discussed later in this work.)

In the four cases where the most agreements and treaties were made in the fourth year, two consisted almost entirely of increases in procedural agreements. This indicates that the theory that the increases would be in agreements that provided goods or those related to military matters was incorrect (see Table 6B). While this phenomenon occurred frequently enough to take note of it, it did not occur with the consistency and prevalency necessary to seek to control for it.

NEWNESS OF THE JOB

Another factor which may have to be controlled for is the fact that, regardless of previous training, a newly elected president requires time to learn the job. Hence I would hypothesize that presidents tend to make fewer agreements and treaties during their first year in office —especially agreements and treaties that provide goods or are military in nature. It is, of course, an oversimplification to state that this "newness" belongs to the president alone. The secretary of state and other foreign policy advisors are also new to their jobs in many cases; furthermore, the president works with other heads of state, and it takes time for them to learn how to deal with the new executive. It should also be pointed out that the president's first year in office is thought to be the time to get things through Congress—the so-called "honeymoon period." This could shift focus away from foreign policy concerns as the administration tries to get domestic legislation passed.

Table 7 shows that Franklin D. Roosevelt, Dwight Eisenhower, and Richard Nixon (if one adjusts his shortened final year to a full year) all made the fewest number of agreements in their first years. (Table 7 only considers presidents who reached office in the normal manner—election. Those who achieved their position through a different manner will be considered in a separate section.) Presidents Carter and Kennedy did not make their smallest number of agreements in their first years. The odds against Presidents Roosevelt, Eisenhower, and Nixon all making the fewest agreements and treaties in their first years simply by chance are 16/10,000 (1/13 × 1/8 × 1/6 = 0.0016).

Table 1 shows that in the three cases where the fewest agreements and treaties were made during the president's first year in office, the first year had 18.6 percent, 23.1 percent, and 26.3 percent fewer agreements and treaties than did the next lowest years of activity. Differences this great again seem to show that the inactivities of the first years were not chance occurrences.

In the cases of Eisenhower and Nixon, the degree of inactivity in foreign policy in their first years in office was caused primarily by the lack of procedural agreements. Once again I am incorrect in hypothesizing that the lack would be in agreements and treaties that either provided goods or were related to military affairs.

It seems clear that presidents do make fewer agreements and treaties during their first year in office. Hence I will have to consider this fact when I try to discern whether presidents use executive agreements to avoid the Senate.

EFFECT OF TRAGEDY

When a person becomes president unexpectedly, due to the death or resignation of his predecessor, how is the foreign policy performance of the U.S. government affected? Will it be necessary to control for the effects of this phenomenon?

Hypothesis: When a vice president becomes president due to death or resignation, the new executive makes fewer agreements in the first year than the previous officeholder made in the last year in the position.

Hypothesis : Most of this decrease will be in agreements that provide concrete goods and in those related to the military.

As Table 8 shows, this hypothesis is incorrect. Two of the three modern presidents who came into office unexpectedly were more active than their predecessors had been in their last years. Tables 2B and 8B indicate that the hypothesized decrease in agreements promising concrete goods and those related to military matters did not occur.

The surprising degree of activity of the unexpected presidents in their first years raises an interesting question. As Table 9 demonstrates, those presidents who came into office through the electoral process failed in three cases out of four to match the activity of their predecessors' final years in office. The unexpected presidents, however, were more active than their predecessors in two cases out of three. Why did the change to unexpected presidents not produce the lull in activity that came in the first years of the expected presidents? The two most probable reasons are: (1) that all of the unexpected presidents were former vice presidents, and the experience that they attained in this position left them better equipped to fill the position than the newly elected presidents; and (2) that these unexpected presidents retained the previous administration's secretaries of state, and that this provided the experience necessary for so smooth a transition. In trying to determine which of these reasons provides the best explanation, it must be noted (see Table 13) that all of the unexpected presidents retained the secretaries of state of their predecessors —at least for a while. This leaves us with only one case for comparison: John Kennedy's secretary of state in his first year was Dean Rusk, who had been the assistant secretary of state in 1949. Did Rusk's experience prevent the expected decline in the number of agreements that usually occurs when a newly elected president takes office? Table 9 shows that the decline in Kennedy's first year in the number of agreements and treaties made (down 5.1 percent) was the second smallest of the elected presidents. (Jimmy Carter made 1.4 percent more agreements in his first year than Gerald Ford had made in his last.) However, Richard Nixon's 8.1 percent decline was not that much greater than Kennedy's. Regardless of the findings, no judgments can be made from only one case. In John Kennedy's case, having an experienced secretary of state did not seem to make much difference; but the question of why unexpected presidents were more active in foreign policy than newly elected presidents remains unresolved.

STATE OF WAR

When the United States becomes involved in wars and "police actions" (such as Korea and Vietnam), what is the effect upon U.S. foreign policy activity? I would hypothesize that the number of agreements and treaties made increases during the times when the United States is involved in prolonged military conflict. (This increase should be primarily in agreements related to military matters and those that provide material goods.)

Table 1 shows that while World War II did generate an increase in foreign policy activity, the degree of activity continued to increase after the war. Table 12 confirms this, and it also shows that U.S. involvement in Korea and Vietnam also failed to produce either consistent or substantial increases in the number of agreements and treaties being made.

However, one could almost chart U.S. entry into World War II and the Korean War by the increases in the percentages and numbers of military-related agreements and agreements that provided concrete goods, as is shown by Table 12B. There are increases to indicate the approach of and entry into each of these wars, and decreases after they are over. In the case of Vietnam, however, the types of agreements made do not reflect the ever-increasing U.S. involvement in Indochina. There was, however, a decrease in the percentages of military-related agreements in the years after South Vietnam fell. This decrease may be due to the fact that there were no more agreements with Vietnam, or it may be a reflection of U.S. "distaste" for military-related agreements with any nation after the bad experience in Vietnam.

THE INFLUENCE OF THE INDIVIDUAL

One factor that cannot fully be controlled for is the influence of the individual. The reason for this is that the influence of an individual cannot fully be measured unless one can substitute other individuals in the same position at the same point in time. Obviously, this cannot be done for U.S. presidents.

The fact that I chose 1933, the year that Franklin Delano Roosevelt assumed office, as a dividing line in time indicates that I believe the individual who occupies the Oval Office should be a critical factor. Franklin D. Roosevelt is, after all, considered to be the father of the modern presidency by many political scientists and historians.

I am certainly not alone in the belief that the individual does matter. James David Barber's *The Presidential Character* revolves around the idea that the character of a president will determine his course of action, and that his actions will have a profound influence upon the nation. Obvious though this may seem, there are some political scientists who believe that it is the role in which a person is placed, more than the person's attitudes and beliefs, that will determine his actions. According to Barber, all of the post-1933 presidents were active except for President Eisenhower. However, if the number of executive agreements and treaties made during a president's term in office is used as an indicator of foreign policy activity, a very different conclusion becomes apparent. Table 4 shows that President Eisenhower was more active in foreign policy than were Presidents Roosevelt, Truman, Johnson, and Nixon. Thus the Barber conclusion does not apply here.

Another example of what may be a popular misconception is the relative willfulness of President Theodore Roosevelt. Arthur Schlesinger, Jr., a noted historian, stated in *The Imperial Presidency* that "when Theodore Roosevelt became President in 1901, the executive agreement rushed into its own" (p. 87). The numbers, however, do not confirm this argument. President Roosevelt averaged seven agreements per year, while his predecessor, McKinley, averaged 5.8 and his successor, Taft, averaged 4.3 (see Table 1). Dr. Schlesinger might argue that his statement did not simply consider the agreements made but also their importance. However, President Roosevelt's agreements with Japan, which allowed Japan to have "influence" in Manchuria and Korea, and with Santo Domingo, allowing for U.S. control over its customs houses, do not seem to be any more important than President McKinley's. McKinley used executive agreements to negotiate an armistice in the Spanish-American War and to develop the Open Door Policy in China.

However, if one combines the number of executive agreements made by a president with the number of treaties negotiated, then President Theodore Roosevelt's popularly acclaimed degree of activity seems to be a fact. Theodore Roosevelt averaged 21.9 agreements and treaties per year as compared to 11.4 for McKinley and 11.3 for his successor, William Howard Taft.

Franklin Delano Roosevelt is another president thought to have been extremely active in foreign policy. However, if we compare Roosevelt's nine years in office *before the United States became involved in World War II*, then he appears to be no more active than his predecessor, Herbert Hoover. Hoover averaged 39.5 agreements and treaties per annum to FDR's 42.2 in his nine years before World War II. When the treaties and agreements made during World War II are added in, however, FDR's average goes up to 64.1. (Roosevelt averaged 115.5 agreements and treaties per year during the war years as compared to the aforementioned 41.2 before the United States became formally involved in the war.)

It is quite obvious that we should not judge presidents (or anyone else) on anything less than hard evidence. However, how can we evaluate the influence of individuals in cases where each individual is in a unique situation, a unique period in time? It is possible to control for certain factors such as party affiliation, whether there is a state of war in existence, and so forth, and comparisons can be made with predecessors and successors. Both of these are done in this study, but the uniqueness of each president remains a factor that cannot be fully controlled for. Theordore Roosevelt was willing to ignore the Senate on controlling the Santo Domingo customs houses, and it is quite possible that other presidents of that era would not have been so willful; but we really do not know.

INFLUENCE OF THE TARGET NATION

What is the influence of the target nation or area, the nation or area with whom the agreement or treaty is being made?

Hypotheses:
1. The percentage of all agreements and treaties made with Western Europe should decline over time as the relative importance of Western Europe has declined.
2. The percentage of all agreements and treaties made with Third World nations (Africa, Asia, and Latin America) should increase over time as they become relatively more important. (This should be especially true for Africa and Asia, where many new nations have come into existence within the past 30 years.)
3. As the Cold War atmosphere subsided, the percentage of agreements with the Soviet Union and the Eastern bloc should have increased.
4. Democratic presidents since John F. Kennedy should, in the tradition of the Peace Corps and the Alliance for Progress, be more active in dealing with the Third World than Republican presidents. Hence a higher percentage of their treaties and agreements should be with Third World nations.
5. The percentage of agreements made with our neighbors, Canada and Mexico, should remain relatively constant over time. This should be the case because most of our dealings with these nations are based upon their proximity, which remains constant over time.

Table 11 (which is taken from Table 10) shows that the first hypothesis is clearly correct. The percentage of agreements and treaties made with West European nations has declined steadily since 1933. This mirrors the decline in relative importance of Western Europe (see Figure 2).

Table 11 shows that the second hypothesis is two-thirds correct. While Asia and Africa have increased in importance (in part because of the increase in the number of nations on these continents), Latin America (not including Mexico), the third member of the Third World, has decreased in importance in U.S. foreign policy. I should have realized that this would be the case. Much of Latin America's importance in the United States' eyes is owing to its proximity. (This is demonstrated by the Monroe Doctrine and the intense efforts of U.S. presidents such as Theodore Roosevelt to enforce it.) Hence Latin America, unlike Africa and Asia, was always important in U.S. foreign policy. As the United States became more involved around the world following the second world war, one would expect a decrease in the relative importance of Latin America.

The third hypothesis, like the first two, seems to be almost self-evident. Therefore, it comes as no surprise that it is also correct. Richard Nixon's trip to Moscow and the establishment of "detente"

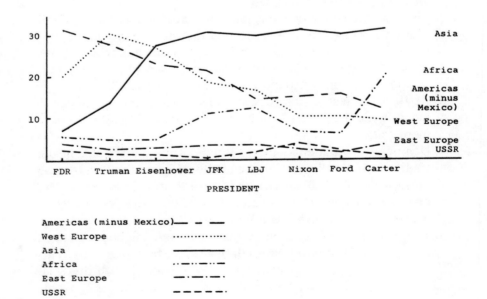

Figure 2. Average Percentage of Agreements and Treaties Made with Each Area by Each President

did lead to a large increase in the number of agreements and treaties between the United States and the Soviet Union. However, I must point out that I expected a much more gradual "thawing out" between these two rivals than proved to be the case.

My fourth hypothesis was based on a belief in Democratic altruism. I took note of the fact that Kennedy had created the Peace Corps and the Alliance for Progress, and that Democratic presidents had been more willing to give the poor a hand domestically than had Republicans since the days of the New Deal. These two facts led me to believe that Democratic presidents would be more active in the Third World than would Republican presidents. This hypothesis only proved to be one-third correct, and altruism seemed to disappear as the motivating factor. Republican presidents were at least as active as their Democratic counterparts in their dealings with Latin America and Asia, but not nearly so active on the continent of Africa. In addition the types of agreements made were the same. One need only note that black citizens are a large portion of the Democratic party, and altruism seems to give way to politics as the motivating factor. (As the number of citizens of Latin American descent who are involved in politics increases, we may see an increase in the dealings of U.S. presidents with Latin American nations. Until very recently, however, the political influence of those of Latin American descent was not nearly as great as that of blacks.)

My final hypothesis was based on a hunch. I assumed that many of the United States' dealings with its immediate neighbors would be over routine matters such as boundary disputes, sharing of facilities, and so forth, and that most of these would be a product of proximity. Since this proximity has remained constant, and neither of our neighbors has become a great military or economic power, I believed that the percentage of agreements and treaties made with our neighbors would remain relatively constant. This has been the case for Canada more than for Mexico, as Table 11 indicates. However, the percentage of agreements and treaties made with Mexico did remain constant from Truman through Johnson. It was only under Nixon, and then Ford, that any substantial changes occurred.

What might be learned that would influence this study? If presidents seem to prefer making executive agreements with certain areas instead of treaties, and it seems that this is being done because of the difficulty that such treaties would have getting through the Senate, then this would confirm that executive agreements are often used to avoid the Senate.

Hypotheses:
1. Presidents would make the lowest ratio of agreements/treaties (more treaties) with nations that are seen as being both *important* and *friendly*, and the highest ratio with nations that are seen as either being unfriendly or unimportant, or both.
2. It follows from hypothesis 1 that the United States should have a higher ratio of agreements/treaties with Eastern Europe after the Soviet occupation, when they came to be seen as hostile nations.
3. It also follows from hypothesis 1 that as Western Europe's importance has declined, the ratio of agreements/treaties has increased.

The reasoning behind hypothesis 1 is that unimportant nations do not merit a treaty to the same degree as important ones, and it would be harder to get a treaty through the Senate if it dealt with an unfriendly nation. Hence the lowest ratio of agreements to treaties should be with Western Europe (seen as being both important and friendly); followed by Mexico and Canada (friendly and moderately important due to proximity); the Americas, Asia, and Africa (less important and less friendly); and the USSR (important but hostile) and Eastern bloc (less important and fairly hostile).

Hypothesis 1 proved to be fairly accurate, as Table 11B demonstrates. Canada, Mexico, and Western Europe did have the lowest ratios of agreements to treaties (and therefore the most treaties per agreement) made with the United States. Contrary to my hypothesis, however, the hostility felt towards the Soviet Union and Eastern Europe (which makes getting a treaty with one of these nations through the Senate quite a task) was not great enough to make the ratio of agreements to treaties higher than those of the "unimportant" Third World areas.

Is the measure that I have chosen to use in this instance (the ratio of agreements to treaties made with a given nation or area) indicative of what I say it is? Does it really reflect how important and how friendly the United States considers a nation or an area to be?

I believe that the fact that Western Europe (with such powers as Great Britain, France, and Germany), Mexico, and Canada had the lowest ratios of agreements to treaties *by far* shows that importance is reflected. (Mexico and Canada are important because of their proximity to the United States.) However, hypothesis 3 did not prove to be correct. There was not a steady increase in the ratio of agreements to treaties as Western Europe's relative importance declined.

The fact that the only nations or areas with whom the United States made *no treaties whatsoever* from the end of World War II until Lyndon Johnson's presidency were the Soviet Union and the Eastern bloc shows that this measure also reflects feelings of amity, or a lack thereof. Even more indicative is the fact that the United States made eight treaties (and 24 executive agreements) with Eastern bloc nations before the Soviet Union took control of them, thus making them "hostile," and no treaties for the 25 years following the Soviet occupation—even though 144 executive agreements were concluded with these nations strongly supporting hypothesis 2.

This last point seems to indicate that presidents do use executive agreements in cases where they believe that the passage of a treaty through the Senate is not feasible. I do not mean to portray the fact that presidents stopped negotiating treaties with the Eastern bloc but nonetheless continued making executive agreements as necessarily an indication that presidents were flaunting the will of the Senate. It may have been infeasible politically for many senators to vote in favor of a treaty with a communist nation, even if the senator personally favored such a treaty. If this were the case, then the usage of executive agreements would be a favor to many senators; nevertheless, the president was still using them to avoid the Senate as a whole.

POLITICAL PARTY

What is the influence, if any, of the political party affiliation of the president?

After World War I came to an end, it was a Democratic president, Woodrow Wilson, who sought to bring the United States into greater involvement in world affairs through the Treaty of Versailles. This treaty, however, was never ratified by the Senate because Republican leaders such as Henry Cabot Lodge and Elihu Root opposed it. The stubbornness of President Wilson, who refused to compromise in any way, and the mutual dislike between Wilson and Henry Cabot Lodge also contributed to the treaty's downfall.

All four of the major bills that ended U.S. isolationism before World War II were pushed by President Franklin Roosevelt, a Democrat, and passed because of overwhelming Democratic party support. The Republicans strongly opposed them as we can see from their voting record (taken from *The Record of American Diplomacy*, edited by Ruhl J. Bartlett, pp. 622-23):

On repeal of the arms embargo:
    Senate: 8 Republicans in favor,   15 against
    House: 21 Republicans in favor, 143 against

On the passage of the lend-lease bill:
    Senate: 10 Republicans in favor,   17 against
    House: 24 Republicans in favor, 135 against

On the adoption of the Selective Service Act:
    Senate: 7 in favor, 10 against
    House: 46 in favor, 88 against

On extension of the period of training:
    Senate: 7 in favor,   13 against
    House: 21 in favor, 133 against

It was a Democratic president, John F. Kennedy, who converted Senator Hubert Humphrey's idea of a peace corps into a reality.

These events led me to the hypothesis that:

Democratic presidents seek more involvement in world affairs (make more executive agreements and treaties) than do Republican presidents.

Table 4 indicates that this hypothesis is incorrect. The three least active modern presidents in foreign policy are all Democrats: Roosevelt, Truman, and Johnson. During the years when Democrats were in the White House, the average number of treaties and agreements made per year was 165. If we leave out the earliest of the modern presidents, Franklin Roosevelt, then the average goes up to 234. However, even this pales before the 250 agreements and treaties made per year by Republican presidents.

What about the types of agreements that were made? Having hypothesized that Democratic presidents are more generous to other nations, I would expect them to make a higher percentage of agreements that provide material goods; and considering the Whig-Republican penchant for choosing presidential candidates with a military background, I hypothesize that Republican presidents made a higher percentage of agreements that were related to military matters. Table 2B provides data which show that one of these two hypotheses was correct. Republican presidents made 14.2 percent defense-related agreements and treaties as compared to 12.1 percent for the Democrats; but the Republicans also made a higher percentage of agreements and treaties that provided material goods: 37.6 percent, compared to 35.5 percent for the Democratic presidents. The most significant finding is the *lack* of difference in these percentages. The political party affiliation of the president seemed to have very little effect on the types of agreements and treaties that were made.

INFLUENCE OF THE SENATE

In at least two cases in U.S. history, the annexations of Texas and Hawaii, it was quite apparent that executive agreements were used in place of treaties because ratification by two-thirds of the Senate seemed doubtful at best. Do presidents use executive agreements with greater frequency when they feel that Senate ratification will be difficult to obtain? To test this, I propose the hypothesis that:

Presidents will have a higher ratio of executive agreements to treaties when the Senate is controlled by the opposition party than they will when their own party controls the Senate.

This hypothesis proved to be correct. When the president and the majority of senators were of the same party, the president negotiated an average of 20.4 agreements for each treaty. When the president and the majority of senators were of different parties, then the president concluded an average of 23.98 agreements for each treaty (see Table 5). There is obviously a difference, but how significant is it? The Mann-Whitney test indicates that there is a 20 percent chance that this difference could have occurred by chance. While this obviously means that there is an 80 percent chance that it did not, this does represent a fair degree of doubt.

Earlier in this work, I mentioned that I would have to look at the effect of the fact that newly elected presidents made fewer agreements and treaties in their first year. It turned out, however, that the ratio of agreements to treaties in each presidential year was almost the same for the five elected presidents' first years (15.7 agreements per treaty) as it was during their first years in office (15.1). Hence I will not have to adjust my figures (control) for this factor.

What difference did it make if the Senate was controlled by the party differing from the president's? What influence did this have on the types of agreements that were made? Data from Table 2B show that the difference is nil. When the president's party constituted a majority in the Senate, 50.7 percent of the agreements and treaties made were procedural, 35.7 percent gave out material goods, and 13.5 percent were related to the military. When the Senate was controlled by the opposition party, 50.3 percent were procedural, 37.3 percent gave out goods, and 12.3 percent were related to the military.

THE BEST TEST

The passage of a treaty actually requires two-thirds of the Senate rather than a simple majority. If presidents really do utilize executive agreements with greater frequency when they believe Senate ratification will be difficult to obtain, then the ratio of agreements to treaties should be significantly lower when the president's party includes two-thirds (or more) of the members of the Senate.

Hypothesis:

Presidents will have a lower ratio of executive agreements to treaties when the Senate has two-thirds (or more) of its members in the president's party.

This hypothesis proved to be correct. When the president's party possessed two-thirds of the seats in the Senate, the president negotiated an average of 13.7 agreements for each treaty. When the president's party did not possess two-thirds of the Senate seats, then the president concluded an average of 24.4 agreements per treaty (see Table 5). The Mann-Whitney test indicates that there is less than *one chance in a million* that this difference occurred by chance. It must be noted that out of the 12 years in which the president's party possessed a two-thirds majority in the Senate, 8 of these were during Franklin Roosevelt's presidency. Many of these years had very low agreement/treaty ratios, which should call into question my findings. Did FDR make fewer agreements per treaty because his party so dominated the Senate, or because he was just following the practices of his predecessors? FDR had very high ratios of agreements/treaties later in his presidency, when he undertook the unpopular course of getting the United States into the second world war. This shows that he was quite willing to use executive agreements to avoid the Senate when he considered this necessary.

This chapter indicates that presidents do use executive agreements to avoid having to get a treaty passed by a two-thirds majority in the Senate. Executive agreements have become the tool by which our government conducts foreign policy for many reasons: besides being easier to conclude, most are routine, some are within the president's power as commander-in-chief, and so forth. Hence the treaty process, the Constitution's main safeguard against presidential excesses in foreign policy, is no longer much of a constraint. What, if anything, stands between the president and complete control over U.S. foreign policy?

5

THE CONSTITUTION
AND THE COURTS

The Constitution is the framework of the U.S. system of government. The powers of the federal government in general, and those of the Congress and the president in particular, all spring from this document. Even a law which has been passed by both houses of Congress and signed by the president can be declared null and void by the courts if it goes against the precepts of the Constitution. What, then, does the Constitution say about treaties and executive agreements, and how have the courts interpreted relevant phrases in this supreme law of the land?

Article II, Section 2 of the Constitution states that the president "shall have Power, by and with the Advice and Consent of the Senate, to make Treaties, provided two-thirds of the Senators present concur." The limitation that would be provided by the Senate seemed in keeping with the Constitutional idea of a separation of powers in that it would deny the chief executive the exclusive treaty-making power that was enjoyed by the monarchs of Europe. Indeed, in his attempts to secure the ratification of the Constitution, Alexander Hamilton stressed this point in *The Federalist* Number 69:

> The President is to have power, with the advice and consent of the Senate, to make treaties, provided two-thirds of the senators present concur. The king of Great Britain is the sole and absolute representative of the nation in all foreign transactions. He can of his own accord make treaties of peace, commerce, alliance, and of every other description.... In this respect, therefore, there is no comparison between the intended

power of the President and the actual power of the British sovereign. The one can perform alone what the other can only do with the concurrence of a branch of the legislature.

While Hamilton probably was not happy with this argument (he had wanted Washington to become a hereditary monarch, the king of the United States), he realized that such a statement was necessary to assuage the fears of the U.S. people with respect to the fact that the Constitution concentrated so much power in the hands of one individual—the president: "Their own colonial experience and their Whig theory of politics had taught them [the Americans] only too well where the source of despotism lay. 'The executive power,' said a Delaware Whig, "is ever restless, ambitious, and ever grasping at increase of power.' "[1] Whether Hamilton meant what he said is irrelevant, because his arguments have come to be accepted as valid interpretations of the intentions of the Constitution.

In contrast to the widely discussed treaty, the word "agreement" appears only once in the Constitution, in Article I, Section 10, paragraph 3, where it is stated that no state shall "enter into any Agreement or Compact with another State, or with a foreign Power" without the consent of Congress. Since the states are forbidden to enter into "any treaty, alliance, or confederation" by the Constitution, but permitted to enter into "agreements or compacts" with the consent of Congress, the Constitution clearly recognizes that there can be international agreements that are not treaties. It is never stated, however, that such agreements can be made by the president, or that such agreements can be made by anyone without the consent of Congress.

One look at the Articles of Confederation, the document which served as the framework of U.S. national government from 1781 to 1789, when the Constitution was ratified, reveals the source of state power to make agreements with the consent of Congress. Article VI of the Articles of Confederation stated that, "No State without the consent of the United States in Congress assembled, shall send any embassy to, or receive any embassy from, or enter into any conference, agreement, alliance or treaty with any king, prince or state." This makes it clear that the authors of the Constitution were simply allowing some of this state power to carry over into the Constitution when they chose to permit states to enter into "agreements or compacts" with the consent of Congress. In no way was this power to make agreements other than treaties to be extended to anyone or anything other than the states themselves.

Why, then, have the interpreters of our Constitution—the courts —allowed executive agreements to be made right and left? Why is it that the Supreme Court allowed a contemporary president to do something that many judges and political scientists believed went against the Constitution itself? That is the topic for the next section of this chapter.

COURT CASES

The law is like a patchwork quilt. It is made in bits and pieces with some of the pieces seeming not to fit.

The battle between the president and Congress for control over U.S. foreign policy also involves a third party. Uninvited though it was by the Constitution, the president, and the Congress to join in this fray, the Supreme Court, nonetheless, ruled in the case of *Marbury* v. *Madison* (1803) that "It is emphatically the province and duty of the judicial department to say what the law is."[2] This decision established the courts as interpreters of the Constitution and subsequent laws. In other words, questions of constitutionality would be decided in courts of law. (One could argue that the first case where the Court decided what the law said was *Ware* v. *Hylton*. In this case, a debt, owed before the Revolutionary War by a colonist to a British subject, was during the war paid into the loan office of Virginia, in pursuance of a law of that state of December 20, 1777, sequestering British property and providing that such payment should discharge the debt. The Court held that Virginia could make such a ruling, because before the Articles of Confederation went into effect, each state had the powers of an independent nation. However, the peace treaty with Britain had nullified the Virginia law and revived the debt.)

By subjecting Constitutional questions to the legal process, the courts assured that we would rarely get clear and comprehensive answers because interpretations accumulate in a piecemeal fashion. First, the courts accept only those cased filed by an affected party. The plaintiff must be able to show that he or she has been harmed in some way, or the court will take no action whatsoever. Second, since the sole aim of the judges is to resolve the case before them, their decision is usually quite narrow, meaning that it is aimed specifically at the question before them, not at establishing broad guidelines for future actions. Third, judges are not immune to public mores. As the standards of society evolve, so do the standards that judges apply to their decisions. Therefore, even though past precedents are usually followed (in the tradition of English common law), judicial interpretation of the law does change over time. Sometimes the change is dramatic: in 1896 the Supreme Court ruled that the doctrine of "separate but equal" (with respect to blacks and whites) was constitutional, only to reverse this decision directly in 1954. Hence legal questions are answered in a piecemeal fashion; and since social mores are constantly changing, the answer is never complete.

The relevance of this chapter to our present day political system becomes all too apparent when we view the court cases that arose as a result of the Iranian hostage situation and the events that followed. On November 4, 1979, the U.S. Embassy in Tehran, Iran, was seized, and over fifty U.S. citizens were captured and held hostage. In response to this crisis, President Carter, in accordance with the International Emergency Economic Powers Act, "declared a national emergency on November 14, 1979, and blocked the removal or transfer of 'all property and interests in property of the Government of Iran, its instrumentalities and controlled entities and the Central Bank of Iran which are or become subject to the jurisdiction of the United States.'"[3]

On January 20, 1981, the U.S. hostages were released pursuant to an agreement concluded on the previous day. This agreement stated that "it is the purpose of [the United States and Iran] ... to terminate all litigation as between the Government of each party and the nationals of the other, and to bring about the settlement and termination of all such claims through binding arbitration"[4] (by an Iranian-U.S. claims tribunal). In short the agreement denied U.S. citizens the right to redress their grievances against Iran in U.S. courts. Instead, it would be up to the joint tribunal to resolve these conflicts.

At least 80 court cases arose from these events. Those most relevant to the questions surrounding executive agreements are discussed here.

Chas. T. Main International, Inc. v. *Khuzestan Water & Power Authority*, 651 F. 2d 800 (1981)

Chas. T. Main International, Inc., was a U.S. engineering firm that brought suit against an Iranian water and power company to attain payment for services rendered with regard to Iranian electrification projects. Following the hostage release agreement, the plaintiff filed suit against the U.S. government, claiming that this agreement exceeded the president's authority in that it "effected a 'taking' of plaintiff's property in violation of the Fifth Amendment."

The Court of Appeals ruled that the International Emergency Economic Powers Act of 1977 provided that the president could void the "exercising (by any person of) any right, power or privilege with respect to . . . any property in which any foreign country has any interest."[5] Hence the president could legally override judicial remedies. "Equally plainly, the compensation clause of the fifth amendment of the Constitution does not constrain the President in nullifying Main's attachments. Main's argument based on the compensation clause is undercut by the fact that its "interest" in Iranian assets was *ab initio* subordinate to the President's IEEPA powers."[6]

The court had ruled that when the president acts "pursuant to an express or implied authorization of Congress, his authority is at its maximum." "In these circumstances, and in these only, may he be said (for what it may be worth) to personify the federal sovereignty. If his act is held unconstitutional under these circumstances, it usually means that the Federal Government as an undivided whole lacks power."[7]

Electronic Data Systems Corporation Iran v. *Social Security Organization of Iran, et al.,* 508 F. Supp. 1350 (1981)

This case demonstrates the complexities of the law in that the circumstances were almost identical to the Main case, but the decision was in complete opposition.

In the EDS case, Judge Robert W. Porter stated that despite the language of the International Emergency Economic Powers Act, "Congress could not and did not intend to grant the President power to nullify or void valid exercises of the judicial power by Article III Courts."[8] Hence the president could not deny EDS the right to seek redress of its grievances in the U.S. judicial system. Congress could not empower the president to violate the Fifth Amendment.

Dames & Moore v. *Regan,* 101 S. Ct. 2972 (1981)

When there is disagreement among the lower courts, it remains for the Supreme Court to resolve the issue. Thus it was that the Supreme Court agreed to hear the case of *Dames & Moore* v. *Regan.*

In writing the opinion of the Court, Justice William Rehnquist held that:

> [the] President was authorized by [the] International Emergency Economic Powers Act to nullify post-November 14, 1979, attachments and direct those persons holding blocked Iranian funds and securities to

transfer them to [the] Federal Reserve Bank for ultimate transfer to Iran, and

[the] President did not lack the power to suspend claims of American nationals against Iran and terminate such claims through binding arbitration in an Iranian-U.S. Claims Tribunal.[9]

According to Judge Porter, who decided the Electronic Data Systems case, this decision would allow the president to violate the Fifth Amendment right of all U.S. citizens to seek redress of their grievances in the U.S. judicial system. Were the courts always willing to allow the president so much freedom in foreign affairs and the usage of executive agreements? If not, then how did they arrive at this position?

Watts v. *U.S.*, 1 Washington Territory (N.S.), 288 (1870)

In 1869 a U.S. citizen named Watts was indicted by a U.S. grand jury for the crime of murdering another U.S. citizen. The alleged homicide had taken place on San Juan Island, a disputed piece of territory, and this proved to be the sticking point.

At the time of the homicide, both the United States and Great Britain claimed this island off the coast of Washington Territory. In 1859 these governments had entered into a convention providing for joint military occupation of the island until the ownership issue was resolved. It was the military which had arrested Watts and turned him over to a U.S. federal district court for trial. (The convention between the United States and Britain excluded Washington Territorial officials from exercising any authority over the area in question.)

After Watts' conviction, his case was appealed with the primary point of contention being one of jurisdiction. Should this case have been tried in a U.S. federal district court? The opinion of the Court, written by Associate Justice Greene, held that the United States government did have the power to make an executive agreement for administration over the island because "no question of state rights or state sovereignty intervenes," and "the power to make and enforce such a temporary convention respecting its own territory is a necessary incident to every national government, and inheres where the executive power is vested."[10]

Associate Justice Greene did make it clear, however, that such "conventions" were not treaties, and therefore not the supreme law of the land. Still, executive agreements were valid within a court of law as long as they did not supercede state sovereignty, even though they lacked the all-encompassing powers of a treaty.

Cotzhausen v. Nazro, 107 U.S. 215 (1882)

The International Postal Treaty of Berne of October 9, 1874 (which was actually an executive agreement), stated that dutiable goods could not lawfully be imported in the mail. Articles so introduced were "liable to seizure" by the customs officers.

In 1882 a woolen scarf valued at $4.00 came in a closed envelope to Milwaukee from Germany. The Milwaukee customs officer, Nazro, had been notified to be present when the envelope was delivered to and opened by the plaintiff (Cotzhausen). Nazro seized the scarf, and it was forfeited to the United States. (The fact that the customs officer had been alerted in advance seems to indicate that these events may have been manufactured in order to produce a test case.) The court ruled that the seizure was in order, indicating that the postal agreement did have the force of law.

Jones v. U.S., 137 U.S. 202 (1890)

In 1890 Henry Jones killed Thomas Foster on Navassa Island, an uninhabited island in the Caribbean sea, which Jones claimed was not a part of the United States. Had Jones been correct, then the United States would not have had jurisdiction over his crime.

At the trial, the government offered as evidence certified copies of letters from State Department files which showed that a U.S. citizen had landed on this uninhabited island in 1857, and had claimed it for the United States. The secretary of state had recognized this citizen's right to the guano on Navassa Island. So even though the president had never made the island a part of the United States, the secretary of state had extended the "laws of the Constitution" (U.S. legal protection) to the island.

The significance of the case for executive agreements was that the court's decision established that "who is sovereign, *de jure* or *de facto*, of a territory is not a judicial, but a political question, the determination of which by the legislative and executive departments of any government conclusively binds the judges, as well as all other officers, citizens and subjects, of that government."[11]

Field v. Clark, 143 U.S. 649 (1892)

In 1892 duties were assessed and collected on various fabric goods imported by Marshall Field and Company, according to the rates established by the Tariff Act of October 1, 1890. Marshall Field and other importers protested against the tax on the grounds that the agreement which brought it into effect was not a law of the United States.

In the Tariff Act of 1890, Congress had stated that the president could levy tariffs on imported goods coming into the United States from nations that had placed a tariff on the same goods exported to them from the United States, and that the president could take such action whenever he felt that it was necessary. Hence the plaintiffs claimed that Congress had delegated both legislative and treaty-making powers to the president in a manner not in keeping with the Constitution.

Mr. Justice Harlan, however, stated in the opinion of the court that "what the President was required to do was simply in execution of the Act of Congress. It was not the making of law. He was the mere agent of the law making department to ascertain and declare the event upon which its expressed will was to take effect."[1][2] The same point was also applied to the objection that this law had delegated treaty-making power to the president.

Underhill v. *Hernandez*, 168 U.S. 250 (1897)

Before discussing this case, I must point out that it is a case dealing with the implications of an act of recognition by the United States government. I am discussing cases dealing with recognition because the Constitution makes recognition a presidential action. The action is an executive agreement in that it confers legitimacy, and other privileges both moral and legal, upon the government that has received recognition. This view will receive further clarification in the court cases that follow.

In 1892 a revolution occurred in Venezuela. The insurrectionists succeeded in taking over the government, and within a month of their victory received recognition from the United States. George F. Underhill was a U.S. citizen who had constructed a waterworks system for the city of Bolivar under a contract with the original regime. When General Hernandez, a revolutionary officer, entered the city at the head of an army, Underhill applied to him, as the officer in command, for written permission to leave the city. Hernandez, however, refused this request and other requests made both by Underhill and by others in his behalf. Finally, Hernandez complied with Underhill's request. (It appears that Hernandez hoped to bully Underhill into continuing to run the waterworks for the new administration.)

Underhill filed suit against Hernandez in 1897 to recover damages for his detention and for certain alleged "assaults and affronts" by Hernandez's soldiers.

The opinion of the court, written by Mr. Chief Justice Fuller, put forward what would become known as the doctrine of state:

> Every sovereign state is bound to respect the independence of every other sovereign state, and the courts of one country will not sit in judgment on the acts of the government of another done within its own territory. Redress of grievances by reason of such acts must be obtained through the means open to be availed of by sovereign powers as between themselves.[13]

This meant that the president and Congress would have to seek redress for their citizens. It would not be done in the courts.

Since the revolutionary government had been recognized by the United States, it was the legitimate government of a sovereign state, and the actions of its military commanders could not have judgment passed upon them in a U.S. court of law. This case did not, however, indicate what would have happened had the revolutionary government *not* been recognized by the United States. The courts take a ruling on a point of law only as far as they have to in order to resolve the case that is before them.

Hawaii v. *Mankichi*, 190 U.S. 197 (1903)

The Hawaiian islands were annexed as a part of the United States through an executive agreement and a joint resolution of Congress, passed on July 7, 1898.

Mankichi filed for a writ of habeas corpus to obtain his release from a Hawaiian prison, where he had been confined for the crime of manslaughter. He claimed that his constitutional rights had been violated in that he was tried upon an indictment not found by a grand jury, and convicted by the vote of nine out of twelve jurors, not the unanimous decision required in the United States. The main point of contention for the court dealt with the time at which the laws of the Constitution went into effect for Hawaii.

The majority opinion of the court argued that annexation established United States sovereignty over that territory, but did not instantly impose U.S. law over the island. The point at which this would occur had to be decided by Congress. The significance of this case for executive agreements was that the court had recognized that an executive agreement approved by congressional joint resolution did establish U.S. territorial sovereignty over an area.

B. *Altman & Company* v. *U.S.*, 224 U.S. 583 (1912)

This case dealt with the right of a tax collector at the port of New York to assess a duty upon a bronze bust imported by B. Altman & Company. The subject of executive agreements came into play in the question of the right of direct appeal to the Supreme Court: "if the reciprocal agreement (made by the President with France) referred to was a treaty within the meaning of section 5 of the circuit court of appeals act, then there was a right of direct appeal to this court."

The Court decided that "matters of such vital importance . . . sometimes involving the peace of nations, should be subject to direct and prompt review by the highest court of the nation"[14] even if the agreement had not been ratified by two-thirds of the Senate. In this particular case, the Supreme Court had decided that an executive agreement merited the same treatment as a treaty.

Oetjen v. *Central Leather Company*, 246 U.S. 297 (1917)

In 1914 two large consignments of hides, allegedly owned by Oetjen's Mexican counterpart company, were confiscated by General Francisco Villa, contrary to the provisions of the Hague Convention of 1907 respecting the laws and customs of war on land. Villa then proceeded to sell the hides to another company, who sold them to the Central Leather Company. Oetjen filed suit in 1917 to regain what the company considered to be its rightful property.

The court ruled that recognition of the Carranza government, whom Villa had served, by the United States made Villa's actions acceptable in the eyes of the courts, even though Villa's actions had been in violation of international law: "the conduct of the foreign relations of our government is committed by the Constitution to the executive and legislative—"the political"—departments of the government, and the propriety of what may be done in the exercise of this political power is not subject to judicial inquiry or decision."[15]

The court took the doctrine of state, put forth in *Underhill* v. *Hernandez*, one step farther: recognition by the United States legitimized all past actions by a regime, even those which were in violation of international law. A redress of grievances for the U.S. company would have to be engineered by the president and/or Congress.

Russian Socialist Federated Soviet Republic v. *Cibrario*, 235 N.Y. at 260 (1923)

This New York state case established that a government recognized by the United States could file suit in U.S. courts.

Conceivably this right (to bring suit) may depend on treaty. But if no treaty to that effect exists the privilege rests upon the theory of international comity. . . . Comity may be defined as that reciprocal courtesy which one member of the family of nations owes to the others. It presupposes friendship. It assumes the prevalence of equity and justice. Experience points to the expediency of recognizing the legislative, executive, and judicial acts of other powers. We do justice that justice may be done in return.[16]

What, however, determines when "comity" exists? "We reach the conclusion, therefore, that a foreign power brings an action in our courts not as a matter of right. Its power to do so is the creature of comity. Until such government is recognized by the United States no such comity exists."[17] The court had ruled that the right of a foreign country to seek redress of grievances in U.S. courts depended upon whether the president had extended recognition to that nation.

Burnet v. *Brooks*, 288 U.S. 378 (1933)

This case does not deal with executive agreements, but with the right of the United States to subject the intangibles of a "nonresident subject of another nation" to a succession tax. However, the case came to have a major influence on the status of executive agreements because of a statement which appears in the opinion of the Court (written by Mr. Chief Justice Hughes): "As a nation with all the attributes of sovereignty, the United States is vested with all the powers of government necessary to maintain an effective control of international relations."[18]

This statement would serve as a precedent in what was probably the most important court case for executive agreements: *U.S.* v. *Curtiss-Wright Export Company*.

U.S. v. *Curtiss-Wright Export Company*, 299 U.S. 304 (1936)

This case does not deal with executive agreements, but it is probably *the* most important case with respect to executive agreements because of the way in which it expanded presidential power. On May 28, 1934, a joint resolution was passed by Congress which stated that the president could legally prohibit through proclamation the sale of arms and munitions to Bolivia and Paraguay, who were then engaged in armed conflict, if such action would "contribute to the re-establishment of peace between those countries."

President Franklin D. Roosevelt took advantage of the joint resolution by proclaiming the prohibition on arms sales to these two Latin

American nations. Thus, when the Curtiss-Wright Export Company was caught conspiring to sell fifteen machine guns to Bolivia, it faced the stiff penalties that had been stated in the joint resolution.

The counsel for Curtiss-Wright, however, argued "that the joint resolution effects an invalid delegation of legislative power to the Executive." Exactly this sort of argument had been dealt with and dismissed in *Field* v. *Clark* in 1892 (discussed above). The Court could have simply cited this case, dismissed the claim of Curtiss-Wright's counsel, and the case of *U.S.* v. *Curtiss-Wright Export Company* would have faded away like so many other cases. The Court, however, chose to go farther—much farther—than they had in *Field* v. *Clark* in delineating why the executive could exercise the powers in question.

Mr. Justice Sutherland wrote the opinion of the Court, and he began by stating that the domestic and the foreign policy powers of the federal government differed "both in respect of their origin and their nature." Whereas the domestic powers given to the federal government by the Constitution had been taken from the individual states, the foreign policy powers had never been held by the states individually, but only by the states as a whole: "And since the states severally never possessed international powers, such powers could not have been carved from the mass of state powers, but obviously were transmitted to the United States from some other source."[19]

The source of these powers was the British Crown. The U.S. government inherited the powers of the Crown (to declare and wage war, to conclude peace, to make treaties, and to maintain diplomatic relations) "as necessary concomitants of nationality," or, one might say, as the birthright of nationhood.

Since the president is the "sole organ of the nation in its external relations," it follows that the president's powers in foreign affairs come from the Crown and not from the Constitution. Hence Justice Sutherland's opinion in *U.S.* v. *Curtiss-Wright Export Co.* did for the president's powers in foreign policy what Chief Justice Marshall's opinion in *McCulloch* v. *Maryland* did for the powers of the federal government: it enhanced them by freeing them from the confines of the strict constructionist viewpoint of the Constitution.

U.S. v. *Belmont*, 301 U.S. 324 (1936)

In 1933 President Franklin D. Roosevelt extended recognition to the government of the Union of Soviet Socialist Republics. It was agreed in the Roosevelt-Litvinov exchange of notes (called the Litvinov agreement) that the claims of U.S. citizens against the Soviet government for U.S. property it had nationalized in 1918 would be dropped. In exchange the Soviet government turned over all the outstanding debts of U.S. citizens to the U.S. government. Hence the U.S. government became the creditor of those U.S. citizens who still owed money to the Soviet Union.

The Petrograd Metal Works had deposited a sum of money with August Belmont, a private banker, prior to the communist takeover. When the Soviet government nationalized this corporation in 1918, the sum of money which had been deposited with Belmont became the property of the Soviet government. Once the debts of U.S. citizens to the Soviet Union were turned over to the U.S. government in 1933, the federal government sought payment from Belmont in 1936.

The opinion of the Court was written by Justice Sutherland, the author of the opinion in *U.S.* v. *Curtiss-Wright Export Company*, and it represented the application of the principles put forward in *Curtiss-Wright* to executive agreements. Sutherland stated that FDR could do what he did with respect to settling the financial situation between the two nations by means of an executive agreement; a treaty was not necessary. In addition the agreement was just as valid in the eyes of the Court as a treaty would have been. The opinion of the Court also stated that recognition of a foreign government legitimizes all acts of such government from the commencement of its existence—not just from when recognition occurs, but from the moment when it comes into existence. This is the case even if the United States disapproved of what the recognized nation did before it was recognized.

U.S. v. Pink, 315 U.S. 203 (1941)

U.S. v. *Pink* was decided by *U.S.* v. *Belmont* in all but one respect. Like *Belmont*, the case involved Soviet funds that had been held by a U.S. citizen in response to the Soviet nationalization of property in 1918, and which became the property of the U.S. government through the Litvinov agreement. *U.S.* v. *Belmont* had established that the conduct of foreign relations is committed by the Constitution to the federal government; that the exercise of that power is not open to judicial inquiry; and that recognition of foreign sovereignty conclusively binds the courts and "is retroactive and validates all actions and conduct of the government so recognized from the commencement of its existence." All of these principles applied to *U.S.* v. *Pink*, but in addition there was the question of state authority. The Supreme Court of the State of New York had taken possession of the assets of the Soviet company, and ordered that they be used to settle the claims of U.S. creditors. In *U.S.* v. *Pink*, the Supreme Court ruled that "state law must yield when it is inconsistent with or impairs the policy or provisions of a treaty or of an international compact or agreement."[20] This decision made the executive agreement equal to the treaty in its supremacy over state law. Like its more formal counterpart, the executive agreement was now the law of the land.

Reid v. *Covert*, 354 U.S. 1 (1956)

Mrs. Clarice Covert (a U.S. citizen) was charged with murdering her husband, a U.S. Air Force sergeant, at an airbase in England. Mrs. Covert, who was a civilian living on the base with her husband, was tried by a court-martial for murder under Article 118 of the Uniform Code of Military Justice. Article 2 of the U.C.M.J. provided for the trial of all dependents by military courts. In addition, at the time of Mrs. Covert's alleged offense, there was an executive agreement in effect between the United States and Great Britain that permitted U.S. military courts to exercise exclusive jurisdiction over offenses committed in Great Britain by U.S. servicemen or their dependents. The Court ruled that neither the U.C.M.J. nor an executive agreement could deny a citizen of the United States the right to a trial by jury as is accorded by the Constitution.[21]

SUMMARY

The courts held in 1870 (*Watts* v. *U.S.*) that executive agreements were not the legal equivalent of treaties, and hence not the supreme law of the land. They were merely "provisional arrangements rendered necessary by national differences" which were entitled to the "respect of the courts."

Cotzhausen v. *Nazro* (1882) established that a postal agreement between two or more nations was enough of a "law" to allow for the seizure of property that was imported in violation of the agreement. It was not until 1912, however, and the case of *B. Altman and Company* v. *U.S.*, that the courts spoke of giving executive agreements the same legal treatment as was received by treaties.

The basis for executive agreements becoming the full equal of treaties was laid in the case of *U.S.* v. *Curtiss-Wright Export Company* in 1936. Justice Sutherland's proclamation that the president's powers in foreign affairs derived from the Crown rather from the Constitution vastly widened the scope of what the president could legally do in the foreign policy arena. In *U.S.* v. *Belmont* (1936), Justice Sutherland stated what *U.S.* v. *Curtiss-Wright Export Company* had only implied: executive agreements were equal to treaties in every way, at least in the eyes of the courts. *U.S.* v. *Pink* in 1941 confirmed the new status of executive agreements by confirming that they, like treaties, have supremacy over state law.

Having come this far, the only remaining limitation for executive agreements is the Constitution. However, remembering Justice Sutherland's opinion in *U.S.* v. *Curtiss-Wright*, which stated that the president's powers in foreign affairs came from the Crown rather than from the Constitution, causes one to wonder just how great a barrier this document will be. In *Dames & Moore* v. *Regan* (1981), the Court was willing to allow President Carter in essence to barter away the property rights of U.S. citizens to be able to settle their claims in the U.S. judicial system in what could arguably be construed as a violation of the Fifth Amendment. This is not to suggest that the courts were in error in this decision; but it does indicate that the courts are no longer firm bastions in the way of presidential actions in foreign affairs. In evolving to the point of equating executive agreements with treaties, the courts have left it mainly up to Congress to restrain (if it so desires) the president's use of executive agreements. As stated before, the law is constantly in a state of flux. The status quo could be changed with one decision, but I doubt that the Court will soon drastically reverse itself with respect to executive agreements.

NOTES

1. Gordon S. Wood, *The Creation of the American Republic, 1776-1787* (Chapel Hill: University of North Carolina Press, 1969), p. 135.

2. *Marbury* v. *Madison*, 1 Cranch 137, 1803, at 177.

3. *Dames & Moore* v. *Regan*, 101 S. Ct. 2972 (1981), at 2978.

4. Ibid., at 2979.

5. *Chas. T. Main International, Inc.*, v. *Khuzestan Water and Power Authority*, 651 F. 2d 800 (1981), at 807.

6. Ibid., at 807.

7. Ibid., at 805.

8. *Electronic Data Systems Corporation Iran* v. *Social Security Organization of Iran, et al.*, 508 F. Supp. 1350 (1981), at 1361.

9. *Dames & Moore* v. *Regan*, 101 S. Ct. 2972 (1981), at 2973.

10. *Watts* v. *U.S.*, 1 Washington Territory (N.S.) 288 (1870), at 293-294.

11. *Jones* v. *U.S.*, 137 U.S. 202 (1890), quoted from case summary.

12. *Field* v. *Clark*, 143 U.S. 649 (1892), at 693.

13. *Underhill* v. *Hernandez*, 168 U.S. 250 (1897), at 252.

14. All excerpts from *B. Altman & Company* v. *U.S.*, 224 U.S. 583 (1912), at 600-601.

15. *Oetjen* v. *Central Leather Company*, 246 U.S. 297 (1917), at 302.

16. *Russian Socialist Federated Soviet Republic* v. *Cibrario*, 235 N.Y. 260, at 260.

17. Ibid., at 262.

18. *Burnet* v. *Brooks*, 288 U.S. 378 (1933), at 396.

19. *U.S.* v. *Curtiss-Wright Export Company*, 299 U.S. 304 (1936), at 316.

20. *U.S.* v. *Pink*, 315 U.S. 203 (1941), at 231.

21. *Reid* v. *Covert*, 354 U.S. 1 (1956).

6

FUNDING

THE POWER OF THE PURSE

The power of the purse is self-evident. What could the leader of a nation or the nation itself accomplish without adequate funding? The House of Commons and the commoners that it represented began with only this power, the power to have their grievances redressed before raising the sums requested by the Crown. Today the House of Commons is all-powerful.

The Founding Fathers recognized the importance of controlling the purse. In *The Federalist* Number 58, James Madison wrote that the members of the House of Representatives

> hold the purse—that powerful instrument by which we behold, in the history of the British Constitution, an infant and humble representation of the people gradually enlarging the sphere of its activity and importance, and finally reducing, as far as it seems to have wished, all the overgrown prerogatives of the other branches of the government. This power over the purse may, in fact, be regarded as the most complete and effectual weapon with which any constitution can arm the immediate representatives of the people, for obtaining a redress of every grievance, and for carrying into effect every just and salutary measure.[1]

Since Article I of the Constitution established the appropriations power as an exclusive prerogative of the Congress, presidents would always be limited by the will of Congress in their foreign policy actions, at least in those actions that required funding. Since the extensive use of executive agreements has been often substituted for the exercise of the Senate's treaty-making power, the power of the purse remains Congress's last control over presidential actions in foreign policy. Does this power remain intact, or has it gone the way of treaty making? In the following pages we will show that Congress's hold on the purse strings is loose, to say the least. The quantity of unreported money in the various bureaucratic departments makes it impossible for presidents to undertake and complete projects without even consulting Congress.

There were some cases early in the nation's history where critical situations caused presidents to circumvent Congress's control of the purse. In 1803 President Thomas Jefferson paid France $11.25 million, plus an additional $3.75 million to cover private claims against France, for the whole of Louisiana. Congress had neither authorized the purchase of the whole of Louisiana, nor had it authorized a sum so large. Despite these facts, Jefferson did not submit the purchase to the Senate for approval until after France had received the requested sum.

> In 1861, after the firing on Fort Sumter, and while Congress was adjourned, Lincoln directed his Secretary of the Treasury to advance $2 million to three private citizens, the money to be used for "military and naval measures necessary for the defense and support of the Government. . . ." Lincoln acted without statutory authority, but the regular channels in the Treasury Department had become suspect since many of the officials were Southern sympathizers.[2]

There can be little question that these cases were extreme cases, in which the gravity of the situation legitimized presidential actions not normally acceptable to Congress.

However, it may now be that presidents are both willing and able to circumvent Congress in funding their foreign policy actions in matters that are far less vital to the national interest.

> By cliche, the power of the purse is now widely referred to as Congress's only remaining lever for redressing the balance between itself and the presidency. Increasingly, Congress is recognizing that its foreign affairs and treaty-making functions are mere ornaments, and that its traditional checks on the Executive are either unrealistic or meaningless. What is left is the appropriations power, and a handful of senators and representatives are invoking it in a muted but growing struggle to revive congressional strength.
>
> Few appreciate, however, the extent to which even the power of the purse, that bulwark of legislative authority, is already controlled by

the presidency. As Congress attempts to tame the Executive by threatening to cut off funds for things like war, it finds that the Executive has already developed innumerable devices for getting the money anyway.[3]

It seems that attempts by presidents to avoid Congressional oversight of their spending practices became much more commonplace with the birth of the modern presidency. (Why one might expect this will be discussed in the next chapter.) This can be seen in the following five examples, each from a different administration.

"In 1933 . . . Franklin D. Roosevelt directed $250 million from funds under the National Recovery Act, a piece of legislation designed to aid the domestic economy during the Great Depression, for a new shipbuilding program."[4]

During the summer of 1950, Yugoslavia suffered a drought. Having split with Stalin, Tito sent his foreign minister to the United States to ask for aid. Dean Acheson, the secretary of state, wrote:

> I warned Kardelj [Yugoslavia's foreign minister] that we could not take on a major Yugoslav financial program because of the ideological problems it would raise for him and us, but must muddle through with bits and pieces for the time being and such help as we could inspire in Europe. The result was not too bad. From the Marshall Plan Authority (ECA) and Export-Import Bank we got together something over thirty million dollars for wheat and induced Congress to switch fifty million dollars previously appropriated for ECA to relief for Yugoslavia.[5]

Note that $30 million would have been provided despite the fact that Congress had not appropriated money for Yugoslavia.

> In 1953, unknown to Congress and using the mutual defense agreement as a cover, President Dwight D. Eisenhower started subsidizing the Ethiopian army in exchange for a major National Security Agency installation at Asmara; this aid led to expansion of Ethiopia's army and a secret commitment to protect the government even from internal threats.[6]

> The contingency fund in the foreign assistance appropriations bill ranged from $155 million to $275 million from fiscal years 1959 to 1963. During that period President Kennedy issued an Executive Order establishing the Peace Corps. Not until seven months later did Congress appropriate funds for the agency. In the meantime, the President financed Peace Corps activities by using more than a million dollars in contingency funds from the Mutual Security Act.[7]

> [O]f the $25 million appropriated for the contingency fund for fiscal 1973, President Nixon utilized $10 million (or 40 per cent) for the "Bahamas Livestock and Research Project." The project was never presented to the committee (in Congress) for funding, either as a grant or a

loan. A committee inquiry failed to produce evidence that the project was urgent, that it was unforeseen, or (as required by the Foreign Assistance Act) "determined by the President to be important to the national interest."[8]

These examples deal with five different administrations and come from four different sources. They are listed to show that (1) political scientists and historians have found cases where presidents funded their actions even though Congress had neither authorized nor appropriated funds for the purpose for which they were utilized; and (2) these cases were not undeniably necessary and vital for our national interest. (Other examples of this phenomenon will appear throughout this chapter, demonstrating that these examples are not isolated incidents but a fairly common practice.) If five presidents were both willing and able to fund actions that Congress did not consider vital to our national interest, then Congress's hold on the purse strings is quite loose indeed; and presidents have a far greater degree of flexibility in their foreign policy actions than was previously suspected.

How is it that presidents are able to fund actions for which Congress has neither specifically authorized nor appropriated funds? The methods used are transfers between accounts, reprogramming, covert financing, secret funds, use of excess stocks, the usage of unexpended funds, the leasing of materials, the forgiving of loans on materials, and the usage of Public Law 480 (agricultural) goods.

TRANSFERS BETWEEN ACCOUNTS

Transfers between accounts occur when agency officials take money from one appropriation account and place it in another. Current law says that except "as otherwise provided by law, sums appropriated for the various branches of expenditures in the public service shall be applied solely to the objects for which they are respectively made, and for no others."[9]

However, in April of 1970, President Richard Nixon announced that he was sending U.S. forces into Cambodia to destroy communist sanctuaries near the border of South Vietnam. This action was financed initially by the transfer of funds from foreign assistance accounts. After his intervention in Cambodia, President Nixon requested $255 million from Congress to provide military and economic assistance to South Vietnam. One hundred million of those dollars was used to restore funds that the president had *already* diverted to Cambodia from other programs.[10]

President Nixon had been able to obtain the $100 million because:

Section 610 of the Foreign Assistance Act allowed him [the president] to transfer up to 10 per cent of the funds from one program to another, provided that the second program was not increased by more than 20 per cent. Furthermore, Section 614(a) of the Foreign Assistance Act gave the President additional authority to spend funds for mutual security whenever he found it "important to the security of the United States." Also, Section 506 gave the President a $300 million emergency fund for military aid. . . . Acting under the first two authorities, President Nixon borrowed $40 million from aid programs originally scheduled for Greece, Turkey, Taiwan, and the Philippines; used another $50 million in funds that had been assigned largely to Vietnam; and diverted still other amounts until a total of $108.9 million in military assistance had been given, or committed, to Cambodia.[11]

Section 506(a) authority (the emergency fund for military aid) played a major role in U.S. aid to Indochina, as Chart 1 indicates.[12]

Chart 1 Section 506(a) Authority

Fiscal Year and Nation	Dollars (millions)
1965, Vietnam	$ 75
1966, Vietnam	300
1974, Cambodia	200
1974, Cambodia	50
1975, Cambodia	75

The willingness of members of the executive branch to transfer funds in a questionable manner and risk the wrath of Congress is quite apparent in the following dialogue. Mr. Daniel Parker, administrator of the Agency for International Development, appeared before the Subcommittee on Foreign Operations of the House Appropriations Committee in 1974 to request additional funding. Mr. Parker wanted an additional $114 million to give to Vietnam. Since he knew that Congress was hostile towards this, he only asked for $54 million, stating that he would transfer the other $60 million out of other Agency for International Development areas.

Mr. Passman (Congressperson from Louisiana):
   "The committee wants to be fair in considering this supplemental request. You do place a very high priority upon the $114 million."

Mr. Parker:
"Yes, sir."

Mr. Passman:
"And what you plan to do is to find $60 million in other program areas from previously appropriated funds and combine this with the $54 million supplemental to total $114 million."

Mr. Parker:
"Yes, sir."

Mr. Passman:
"Do you feel it is important enough to have $114 million for Vietnam even at the expense of displeasing members of Congress, that the priority is high enough that you would take it from other areas and take your chance on a subsequent reprimand?"

Mr. Parker:
"Yes, sir. I believe that world peace is very importantly at stake in Vietnam."[13]

The transfer of funds from one appropriations account to another may deplete an account. Individuals in the executive branch, however, may be clever enough to take funds from an account which Congress will have to replenish.

In hearings before the Senate Appropriations Committee for fiscal year 1976, General John A. Kjellstrom, Comptroller of the Army, came before the committee to request $120 million in supplemental funding for four overobligated (overdrawn) accounts. General Kjellstrom admitted that during the fiscal years of 1971-75 $921 million had been transferred out of these accounts. When asked what would happen if Congress were to refuse to appropriate the requested $120 million, the general replied that various unpaid contractors would probably sue the federal government and would receive not only the full amounts owed them but additional damages.[14]

One theme which will become quite apparent throughout this chapter is that the legislative branch has often been a willing partner in the loosening of its control over the purse strings. The example that applies to the transfer of funds is Section 614 of the Foreign Assistance Act, which allows the president to waive requirements of the Act, and transfer funds in any way that seems necessary, whenever such action is "important to the security of the United States." "There were 17 such waivers between July, 1970, and October, 1971, and in none was Congress notified before the fact."[15]

REPROGRAMMING

Reprogramming is the shifting of funds within an appropriation account from one program to another. According to Louis Fisher in *Presidential Spending Power*, the authority for reprogramming is generally nonstatutory. Congresspeople tend to set the restrictions for reprogramming during committee hearings through "gentleman's agreements" with the agency heads. For example, the Appropriations Committee might instruct an agency head not to increase the funds of anything by more than 15 percent of the amount originally allotted.

> Different congressional committees handle reprogramming in their own way. All that is ordinarily required is an informal clearance by four men: the relevant subcommittee chairmen of the House and Senate Appropriations committees and authorizing committees. Often, reprogramming is perfunctorily handled at the staff level by the subcommittee clerks. Sometimes congressmen are polled on the changes, and at best, a closed hearing is held.[16]

In December of 1969, the House Appropriations Committee stated in its military budget report that the Navy was moving "too fast" in approving production of the F-14 fighter before structural tests had been completed. Mindful of the C-5A and the Air Force's error in purchasing 331 F-111's—all lemons—before technical difficulties had been solved, the committee stressed a fly-before-you-buy policy. To ensure this practice, the committee slashed the requested $275 million for purchase of the first six production aircraft, and ordered that "none of the funds provided . . . be utilized for tooling beyond that needed for fabrication of the test aircraft."

The Navy, however, went back to Rep. George Mahon's defense subcommittee in April of 1970, and slipped its reprogramming request into the large pile of other reprogramming requests. In this manner it gained $517 million to build 26 production models despite the original decision of the committee. As is usually the case, no one outside of the subcommittee was informed of this change.[17] "Defense reprogrammings in fiscal 1971 alone involved 132 transfers totaling $3.3 billion. All but 16 were approved."[18]

COVERT FINANCING

Our Founding Fathers recognized the need for secrecy in diplomacy, and in "an act of July 1, 1790, provided $40,000 to the President to pay for special diplomatic agents. It was left to the President to decide the degree to which such expenditures should be made public."[19]

"The term 'confidential funding' . . . refers to the practice of certifying that funds have been spent. A certificate, signed by an authorized official becomes a sufficient voucher and precludes further auditing."[20]

Confidential funds are created in several different ways. The primary method is authorization in substantive legislation, followed by funding in an appropriation act. The authorization is usually for an indefinite period, requiring an appropriation each year. Some authorizations, such as the one for the National Aeronautics and Space Administration, must be renewed each year in legislation.

Confidential funds are sometimes created by the appropriation of expenditures without the support of authorizing legislation. This type of action represents legislation in an appropriation bill, and is therefore in violation of congressional parliamentary procedure. Hence any legislator could raise a point of order against such a fund unless a special rule has been adopted by Congress to protect the fund. A number of such parliamentary challenges have been raised in recent years.

A third type of confidential fund can be created by authorization legislation without specific sums being appropriated for that purpose. The funds are then taken from monies regularly appropriated each year, a portion of which (specified in the authorization legislation) may be spent for confidential purposes. Foreign assistance is often executed in this manner.

If substantive authority for a confidential fund exists, but there has been no mention of funding whatsoever, then authority is latent, contingent on the necessary appropriation.[21]

In "Confidential Funding: A Study of Unvouchered Accounts," a report prepared for the House Budget Committee, Louis Fisher stated (p. 3) that there were 28 separate confidential funds available for fiscal 1977, totaling $23.543 million. This did not, however, include a one-time (not renewed each year, only a lump sum) $50 million authorization for the president in foreign assistance.

> Section 614 of the Foreign Assistance Act of 1961, as amended, authorizes the President to use amounts not to exceed $50 million pursuant to his certification that it is inadvisable to specify the nature of the use of such funds. The certification shall be deemed a sufficient voucher for such amounts. When funds are spent in that manner, the President shall "promptly and fully" inform the Speaker of the House and the chairman and ranking minority member of the Senate Committee on Foreign Re-

lations. 22 U.S.C. 2364(c). The $50 million is a cumulative figure rather than annual authority. Each use of the authority depletes the amount available. If and when the President spends $50 million by certificate, the authority would be exhausted. Congress would then have to decide whether to renew the authority and by what amount.[22]

SECRET FUNDS

Whereas "confidential funds" are cited in appropriation bills (the appropriation is public while the expenditure and auditing are concealed from Congress and the public), secret funding is covert at every stage.

> Political scientist Louis Fisher cites an estimate that in the 1972 fiscal budget of $249 billion, secret funds may amount to $15 billion to $20 billion. No one really knows, for example, in how many different ways foreign assistance is given, nor exactly how much it all adds up to. The only item in the budget clearly marked as military aid totals around $400 million. That is a gross understatement. At Joint Economic Committee hearings last January, Senator William Fulbright introduced a table showing more than $6.9 billion in military assistance and sales for fiscal 1972. Two Defense Department officials broke pencils while disagreeing with each other over the total cost, finally putting the figure at $4.9 billion and later revising it to $6.3 billion.[23]

With so much money available in secret funds, Congressional oversight of executive actions may be difficult at best in many cases.

> Senator Case, member of both the Appropriations and the Foreign Relations Committees, had to rely on an article in the *Christian Science Monitor* to learn that the Administration had agreed to finance Thai troops in Laos. Further investigation by Senate staff members disclosed that the CIA was covertly financing Thai troops fighting in northern Laos. The cost of the operation ran to several hundred million dollars a year. An amendment by Senator Symington, to establish a ceiling of $200 million on U.S. expenditures in Laos during fiscal 1972, had to be raised to $350 million. Symington later said that the secret war in Laos was done without knowledge on the part of members of the Senate Armed Services Committee.[24]

USE OF MILITARY STOCKS

Timothy Ingram wrote in *The Washington Monthly* in January 1972 that estimates of the amount of obsolete weapons and supplies available to the Defense Department for military grant aid alone ran to well over $9 billion in 1972. Since there are no guidelines, a fairly new weapons system can be declared "excess" and then shipped off to any nation that the Defense Department deems needy.

Between January 1977 and February 1982, the U.S. Navy sold 182 ships to foreign governments. The prices for all of these ships were based upon their value as scrap. "The total sales price for these ships equalled $33.8 million, which represents 4.56 percent of the total U.S. acquisition cost of $723.6 million."[25]

In addition "grants of surplus war goods are not listed as current outlays for military aid. Thus, the Departments of State and Defense were able to keep Chiang Kai-shek's forces well stocked with excess aircraft, tanks, howitzers, and M-14's, even though Congress, busily voting reductions in Taiwan's regular military assistance, believed arms shipments were being diminished."[26]

UNEXPENDED FUNDS

Another source of funding for actions that have received neither authorization nor appropriation from Congress is the enormous amount of money which carries over each year, called unexpended authority.

> During floor debate last October [1971] over the Symington ceiling on funds for Laos, Senator Fulbright voiced his suspicions: "I have never figured out how [Defense managers] are able to spend money that has neither been authorized nor appropriated. They have ways of drawing on unexpended funds. I imagine there is at least $50 billion of unexpended funds in the pipeline [slang for unexpended authority] as reserve for the Pentagon. So I would not be sure that even with a prohibition against appropriation of any money, they could not find some in a very short time."[27]

The phenomenon of unexpended authority springs from the concept of full funding. The vast majority of appropriations are for one year only, and the amounts not spent are supposed to be returned to the Treasury. In the case of long-term projects, such as the construction of a large naval vessel, Congress would rather appropriate one large sum that carries over for a specific time until spent. This saves Congress from having to reappropriate an amount each year, and also allows Congress to know from the start how much the project will cost. The setting aside of a specific sum also serves as a ceiling for the cost of the project, at least in theory. The disadvantage of this procedure is that if the project is cancelled or comes in under budget, the remaining funds do not revert to the Treasury.

Having accumulated excess funds "in the pipeline," the branches of the military are careful always to keep something in reserve. For example, in its 1972 budget request, the Army claimed that a $30 million carryover from the previous year was available for a given project involving NATO, when there was actually $40.4 million available.[28] The Army did not report the full amount because one might suspect that they wanted to keep the extra $10.4 million—just in case they needed it for something.

In fiscal 1971, the Defense Department spent $3 billion more than it had been granted by Congress. Accountability is at a minimum, to say the least, in cases where projects can be funded with these excess funds.

LEASES OF EQUIPMENT

In 1977-80, the United States concluded 48 lease arrangements for military equipment with foreign nations having a total value of approximately $80 million. Of this equipment $52.5 million worth was provided on a rent-free basis. For example, six helicopters were leased to El Salvador for one year without charge; a destroyer was leased to Turkey at no charge; and so forth.[29]

Following the recommendation of the General Accounting Office, Congress passed legislation in December 1981, that seeks to prevent rent-free or nominal-rent leases of defense property to foreign governments. It remains to be seen, however, if this law can be enforced.

THE FORGIVING OF LOANS BY THE UNITED STATES

Sections 23 and 24 of the Arms Export Control Act (22 U.S.C. paragraph 2751 *et seq.*) authorized the Foreign Military Sales Financing Program. The Act allows the president to grant direct credit or guaranteed loans to enable foreign governments and international organizations to purchase U.S. defense materiel and services, and to forgive repayment of these credit sales and guaranteed loans for certain countries.[30]

The nation which has benefited the most from this act is Israel. "Direct credits were first forgiven for Israel in Fiscal Year 1974; from FY 1974 through FY 1976 $2.4 billion in direct credits were forgiven."[31] "Recently, repayment of Egypt's direct credits were forgiven; and Egypt and Sudan are also seeking debt forgiveness for fiscal year 1983."[32]

PUBLIC LAW 480

The Agricultural Trade Development and Assistance Act (Public Law 480) authorized the Food for Peace program in 1954. Public Law 480 allows for two types of agricultural commodity assistance: Title I permits long-term credit sales to foreign governments at low interest rates, whereas Title II consists of donations.

In 1973 the General Accounting Office investigated U.S. aid to Korea. GAO found that Public Law 480 concessional sales had been increased and were being used indirectly to offset reductions in another U.S. assistance program. Korea was selling the commodities and using the money for military budget support or economic development, usage which goes against the specifications of the act.[33]

CONGRESS AND CONTROL OF THE PURSE

The ability of the members of the executive branch to find money when they need it is well illustrated by the following staff memorandum on the availability of sources of temporary aid for Cambodia.

Section 614 of the Foreign Assistance Act authorizes the President to give any country that is "a victim of active Communist or Communist supported aggression" up to $250,000,000 in a fiscal year without regard to the regular requirements of the Act, if he deems it "important to the security of the United States." This allows, for example, certain appropriations for economic aid to be used for military aid, as has already been done for Cambodia with $50 million in supporting assistance funds.

Here is a listing of the major sources of additional aid for Cambodia that do not require further Congressional authorization:

1) Draw on Department of Defense stocks of materials and services as authorized by Section 506 of the Foreign Assistance Act ($300,000,000 authorized)—up to $150,000,000 can be used for Cambodia.

2) Transfer certain unobligated economic aid funds for use as military or economic aid under the authority of Section 610 of the Foreign Assistance Act—up to $150,000,000 can be given to Cambodia.

3) Use of unobligated military aid funds (at least half of the 1971 appropriation of $350 million is available)—up to $150,000,000 can be given to Cambodia.

4) Use of excess defense articles, such as from U.S. units leaving Vietnam—no limit.

5) Use of enemy material captured in the Cambodian operation or in Vietnam—no limit.
6) Agricultural commodities under the P.L. 480 program—no limit.[34]

The two most important points of this chapter are that (1) Congress's control over the purse strings has been weakened by the methods discussed; and (2) in large part Congress has either created, or at least consented to, these methods. Congress can place much of the blame on itself for this problem, if it is, indeed, a problem.

Reprogramming, as was stated earlier, usually requires an informal clearance by four people—two senators and two representatives. Do they consult the members of their committees, or at least carefully consider the effects of an affirmative answer, or do they often allow it as a matter of routine? In the Foreign Assistance Act of 1961, Congress granted the president a great deal of discretion in transferring funds between accounts. Congress creates both covert and secret funds. It is no secret to them. Congress has never set strict guidelines on when military equipment becomes "obsolete," so the Pentagon can declare an almost new system to be "obsolete" and give it to someone else. Congress created full funding of long-term projects to save itself work. The existence of unexpended authority, however, allows an agency to do a wide variety of things totally out of the view of Congress. Congress passed legislation permitting the president to forgive loans to certain nations, and it approved Public Law 480. Congress did pass legislation to stop the leasing of equipment without charge, but much more must be done if Congress wants to regain control over the purse strings.

Congresspeople are not stupid. In this case they may have been either lax in their oversight duties or naive in their belief that the executive branch would not take advantage of the discretion that was granted to it. However, they may well have been guilty of *neither* of these charges. They may well have created this situation because they wanted it to work out the way that it has.

NOTES

1. Alexander Hamilton, James Madison, and John Jay, *The Federalist*, Number 58, in *The Federalist Papers*, intro. Clinton Rossiter (New York: The New American Library, Mentor Book, 1971), p. 359.

2. Louis Fisher, *Presidential Spending Power* (Princeton, N.J.: Princeton University Press, 1975), p. 230.

3. Timothy H. Ingram, "The Billions in the White House Basement," *The Washington Monthly*, January 1972, p. 36.

4. Alexander DeConde, ed., *A History of American Foreign Policy* (New York: Charles Scribner's Sons, 1978), 2:99.

5. Dean Acheson, *Present at the Creation* (New York: W.W. Norton and Company, 1969), p. 333.

6. Alexander DeConde, ed., *Encyclopedia of American Foreign Policy* (New York: Charles Scribner's Sons, 1978), p. 342.

7. Louis Fisher, *Presidential Spending Power*, pp. 67-68.

8. Ibid., p. 69.

9. Ibid., p. 104.

10. Ibid., p. 107.

11. Ibid.

12. U.S. House of Representatives Hearings, Before the Subcommittee of the House Appropriations Committee, on the Supplemental Appropriations for Fiscal Year 1977, 95th Congress, First Session, p. 898.

13. U.S. House of Representatives Hearings, Before the Subcommittees of the House Appropriations Committee, on Supplemental Appropriations (Part 2), 93rd Congress, Second Session, 1974, p. 833.

14. U.S. Senate Hearings, Before the Senate Appropriations Committee, on Supplemental Appropriations for Fiscal Year 1976, 94th Congress, 1976, pp. 1038 and 1072.

15. Timothy H. Ingram, "The Billions in the White House Basement," p. 38.

16. Ibid., p. 43.

17. Ibid., pp. 43-44.

18. Ibid., p. 43.

19. Louis Fisher, *Presidential Spending Power*, p. 205.

20. Louis Fisher, "Confidential Funding: A Study of Unvouchered Accounts," prepared for the House Budget Committee, U.S. Government Printing Office, March 1977, p. 1.

21. Ibid., p. 2.

22. Ibid., p. 23.

23. Timothy H. Ingram, "The Billions in the White House Basement," p. 40.

24. Louis Fisher, *Presidential Spending Power*, p. 217.

25. "U.S. Security and Military Assistance: Programs and Related Activities," report by the U.S. General Accounting Office, June 1, 1982.

26. Timothy H. Ingram, "The Billions in the White House Basement," p. 38.

27. Ibid., p. 41.

28. "How the United States Finances Its Share of Contributions to NATO," report to Congress by the Comptroller General of the U.S., 1973.

29. "U.S. Security and Military Assistance: Programs and Related Activities," pp. 42, 44.

30. Ibid., p. 14.

31. Ibid.

32. Ibid.

33. "U.S. Assistance for the Economic Development of the Republic of Korea," report to Congress by the Comptroller General of the U.S., July 12, 1973, pp. 9, 49.

34. U.S. Senate Hearings, Before the Senate Foreign Relations Committee, on Supplemental Foreign Assistance Authorizations, December 11, 1970, p. 86.

7

CONGRESS: A PARTNER IN FOREIGN POLICY?

Over 2,000 years ago Plato discussed the advantages and disadvantages of various forms of government in the *Republic*. Plato's ranking of the forms of government, from best to worst, are shown in Chart 2.

Chart 2 Plato's Rankings of forms of Government

Best form	Philosopher-King	one person rules
	Aristocracy	small group rules
	Democracy	all, or at least a large group, rule
	Oligarchy	small group rules
Worst form	Tyranny	one person rules

It is fascinating to note that both the best and the worst forms of government are rule by one individual. This seems to be almost self-evident because one individual, ruling by fiat, is the most efficient form of rule and could therefore do the most harm or the most good, depending on the individual. It follows that rule by a small group should be both the next best and the next worst forms of government. A small group is not as efficient as rule by one. It takes longer for a small group to agree on a course of action. Indeed, its members may not agree at all, and nothing will be done. Rule by a large group, democracy, is the least efficient form of government. It will probably take a long time to reach a decision, and the chance that there will be no consensus, and therefore no action taken, is much greater. Hence democracy should be considered the *safest* form of government, because no action will be taken unless the need for it and the benefits of it are obvious enough to convince a large group of individuals that it should be done.

This paradigm can easily be transferred to the U.S. foreign policy arena. Rule by one individual, the president, can lead to both the best and the worst forms of government. It is much *safer* if Congress, a large group, is allowed to have a large input into foreign policy decision making. However, I doubt that we can afford to sacrifice efficiency and secrecy in order to ensure domestic safety in the foreign policy arena.

Alexander Hamilton stated the dangers of allowing interference by a large body (the House of Representatives) in the formation of treaties in *Federalist* Number 75:

> Accurate and comprehensive knowledge of foreign politics; a steady and systematic adherence to the same views; a nice and uniform sensibility to national character; decision, secrecy, and dispatch, are incompatible with the genius of a body so variable and so numerous. The very complication of the business, by introducing a necessity of the concurrence of so many different bodies, would of itself afford a solid objection. The greater frequency of the calls upon the House of Representatives, and the greater length of time which it would often be necessary to keep them together when convened to obtain their sanction in the progressive stages of a treaty would be a source of so great inconvenience and expense as alone ought to condemn the project.[1]

Have Hamilton's fears been confirmed? In my opinion they have.

THE INTERESTS OF CONGRESS ARE LOCAL

Richard Fenno (in *Congressmen in Committees*, 1973) delineated the three goals of congresspeople to be reelection, the attainment of power in the House, and the making of good public policy. No matter how one looks at it, neither of the latter two goals is possible without achieving the former. One cannot make good public policies without being in the Congress. One has a much better chance of being able to make good public policy if one is powerful within the body, and power within the body is attained by reelection due to the seniority system. In short, reelection is vital. In order to get reelected, congresspeople must please those they represent. For a member of the House, each district is roughly 1/435th of the national population (450,000 people). Even the senators from California represent less than 10 percent of the total U.S. population. Since their constituents are the key to their reelection, congresspeople may often choose to place their constituency interests over the national interest, and this can have disastrous effects on foreign policy.

George Grassmuck, in *Sectional Biases in Congress on Foreign Policy*, pointed out that Great Plains legislators of both parties in both the House and the Senate opposed a big Army and a big Navy, foreign loans and aid, and repeal of neutrality restrictions, because the Great Plains "built no battleships and manufactured no guns" (p. 162). "As for reducing appropriations which would be spent in other parts of the country, legislators who once united as a farm bloc and who resolutely opposed tariffs protecting Eastern manufacturing found little difficulty in opposing those armament measures bringing advantage to Eastern shipbuilding and arms manufacturing firms."[2] In contrast state delegations that had naval bases, ports, coastlines, and so forth, were much more willing to give money to the Navy.

Another classic example of congressional sectionalism involved the Saint Lawrence Seaway:

> Americans and Canadians had long wanted to improve the navigation channels of the St. Lawrence waterway between Montreal and the Great Lakes by deepening them, and to exploit and share the electric power resources of the St. Lawrence River. In July 1932, the two countries signed the St. Lawrence Seaway Treaty, designed to make the project a reality through a plan of shared costs, but in March 1934, sectional opposition in the United States led to the treaty's defeat in the Senate. . . . Every president since the First World War had supported the idea of the St. Lawrence Seaway, but until 1954 the project had always run into insurmountable opposition in Congress. Powerful special interests, primarily eastern railroads, east coast seaports that feared a diversion of their traffic to lake ports, the coal industry, and power companies fought the seaway and related electrical power projects.[3]

The St. Lawrence Seaway Treaty was defeated in the Senate in 1934, but Franklin D. Roosevelt revived the idea in 1940. In an attempt to circumvent congressional opponents, FDR made an executive agreement with Canada in March 1941, calling for the completion of the St. Lawrence Seaway and related power projects. World War II, however, stalled any further action.

After World War II, Congress still hesitated to act. In 1951, tired of waiting for the United States to act, the Canadians decided to begin construction on their own. Congress finally took action in 1954, and the St. Lawrence Seaway was completed.

Thomas Franck and Edward Weisband, in *Foreign Policy by Congress* stated that the congressional decision to punish Turkey, our most powerful Mediterranean NATO ally, after its 1974 invasion of Cyprus was, in large part, a product of the lobbying by citizens of Greek descent and the presence of large numbers of this interest group in numerous congresspeople's districts:

> The biggest and most successful effort of the Greek organizations and churches was in persuading Congress to punish Turkey after its 1974 invasion of Cyprus. That attack began on August 14; by August 30, Democratic Majority Leader Mansfield was complaining publicly of the avalanch of telegrams from Greek-American organizations urging Congressional action to stop the flow of U.S. arms transfers to Turkey. That an embargo was imposed by Congress against the advice of the President and almost all Congressional leaders of both parties testifies to the effectiveness of a campaign coordinated by Father Evagorus Constantinides and implemented in the House of Representatives by a handful of members of Greek origin who are highly respected for their ability and political acumen.[4]

Early in 1975 (or perhaps as early as July 1974), the Central Intelligence Agency began escalating its involvement in Angola. With Portuguese rule at an end, the CIA sought to transfer its support to Holden Roberto. In addition the USA joined China in aiding UNITA (National Union for the Total Independence of Angola), another faction. The United States' aim was to prevent the MPLA (Popular Movement for the Liberation of Angola), which was supported by the Soviet Union, from gaining control of Angola.

For six months Congress went along. As U.S., Soviet, and Cuban involvement increased, however, memories of Vietnam began to haunt U.S. public opinion and Congress. Numerous congresspeople began working toward a phased withdrawal of the CIA from Angola. However,

> these efforts to effect a phased termination of CIA involvement were suddenly outflanked by Senator Tunney, not a member of the Foreign Relations Committee but a man with a very urgent problem. The Californian was up for reelection in a tight Democratic primary, pitted against anti-war activist Tom Hayden who was backed by his wife Jane Fonda and the Fonda family fortune. As a lackluster Senator, Tunney was in urgent need of instant visibility and an enhanced dove image. Angola came along like the serendipitous answer to an underdog's prayer. ... Thus, in a sense, the Angola War was lost in the California primary.[5]

Such happenings as these are not lost on the members themselves. House International Relations Committee Chairman Zablocki has said, "Congress is too responsive to the lobbies of ethnic and special interests in the U.S. to be able to take the lead in foreign policy-making without endangering the national interest."[6]

Congress's ability to avoid constituency pressure was lessened by the introduction of the electronically recorded vote. Prior to this, the public often did not know how each congressperson had voted on a given bill. Only when roll call votes were taken did the constituents know any more than how many congresspeople had voted for a given proposal and how many had voted against it. Electronically recorded voting told how each congressperson had voted on each issue. Suddenly, hometown newspapers had access to detailed voting records, and each constituent could keep a much closer watch on the actions of his/her congressperson.

THE LACK OF SECRECY IN A LEGISLATIVE BODY

It has been said that something ceases to be a secret when more than one person knows about it. Is it possible for 535 congresspeople to keep a secret? Is secrecy all that necessary in the foreign policy arena?

In 1975 the White House, following a request for modern military equipment from King Hussein of Jordan, directed the Joint Chiefs of Staff to study the military situation in Jordan. The Joint Chiefs urged that Hawk missiles be sold to Jordan so that Hussein would not be tempted to seek assistance elsewhere. Perhaps fearing the Israeli lobby, President Ford sought to keep Congress in the dark until the point at which the law required him to alert the Congress of his plans. Ford had intentionally waited to inform Congress of his actions until right before Congress was to recess for the summer. He had hoped that this would minimize congressional interference.

Hearings were held in both the Senate Foreign Relations Committee and the International Relations Committee of the House, and the merits of King Hussein's regime were openly discussed. This infuriated King Hussein, and he called the whole deal off. Eventually, the arms sale did take place; but it was clear that "these public, often brutal congressional evaluations of foreign nations seeking to do business with the U.S., tend to have the effect of canceling out whatever goodwill the transaction is intended to achieve."[7]

Another example of the effects of Congress's open decision making came after the passage of the 1974 Trade Act. "On that occasion, the Soviet leaders at first agreed to ease barriers to Jewish emigration but finally reneged, after the Congress had made the arm-twisting increasingly public."[8]

A CIA agent was assassinated in Athens "just after leaks from the Pike Committee had enabled various little publications to publish lists of CIA agents overseas."[9]

Under the present system of senatorial oversight over the CIA, the CIA must give the new Senate Select Committee (created by S. Res. 400) 48 hours' notice before commencing a covert action, once the action has received presidential approval.

> If a majority [of the committee] were to decide against a proposed covert action, the chairman would communicate this decision to the [Director of Central Intelligence]. If the director were to persist, the committee chairman could ask the President to intervene. Should he refuse, the committee could call the Senate into executive (closed) session. The Senate could then pass a secret resolution opposing the proposed operation. If that failed to get results, the operation could be debated in open session. "That," Senator Inouye commented, "would make it a public covert operation."[10]

What would happen, however, if a majority of the committee voted against the proposed covert action, but the Senate in executive (closed) session decided to okay the action? Would all 100 senators choose to keep a secret, or would one of the dissenting senators leak the operation to the press thereby undermining the Senate decision?

"President Carter has joined his predecessors in complaining, repeatedly, that Congressional leaks of classified information are damaging national security and that reliable intelligence sources are drying up because they fear the leaking of confidential information they supply."[11]

THE LACK OF FLEXIBILITY IN THE LAW

In June 1978 President Carter complained that "excessive use of legislative vetoes and other devices to restrict foreign policy actions can impede our ability to respond to rapidly changing world conditions. Reasonable flexibility is essential to effective government."[12]

> In 1973—when these tragic events [the fall of Saigon] could not have been foreseen—the Eagleton Amendment to the Foreign Assistance Act

had prohibited any use of U.S. forces in Cambodia and Vietnam.... But in barring all use of funds for any military activities in, over, or off Vietnam, Laos, and Cambodia, the letter of the law also prohibited use of the Marines to evacuate the embassy at Saigon. That Eagleton probably intended no such consequence merely illustrates a hazard of controlling foreign relations with inflexible—and case-specific—legislation.[13]

To evacuate the U.S. embassy, President Ford had no choice but to violate the law.

Law by nature is inflexible. It is to a large degree meant to be inflexible. Congress's attempts to be the president's equal in the foreign policy process via the passage of laws cannot help but decrease the nation's flexibility in foreign affairs.

THE LACK OF SPEED

Hand in hand with flexibility goes the ability to act with speed. The faster that one can act, the later one can wait to act, thus keeping options open. Congress is notorious for its inability to act rapidly. "The process of inquiry, discussion, and debate in the legislature is inherently ill-adapted to speed."[14] At the outbreaks of both the War of 1812 and the Civil War, Congress was still debating whether to allocate the funds necessary for adequate national defense. Neither war was a surprise, but Congress still failed to make the judicious decisions before they were forced to. How could 100 senators bargain with the Soviets over a new SALT treaty? The Soviets might have made an offer, and by the time the Senate framed an answer Brezhnev and other Politburo members have passed away. In this age of "mutually assured destruction," which can be executed, so to speak, in a matter of minutes, the dilatoriness of Congress make it well nigh impossible for this body or any of its components to be a viable partner in critical foreign policy decision making.

THE COMMITTEE SYSTEM

The very structure of Congress makes it an irrational and inefficient decision maker. First, the decentralization of power into committees and subcommittees has made congressional policy making less rational in that the majority cannot always get what it wants. Bills can get stuck in subcommittees or committee, or be filibustered by one individual on the floor of the Senate. Second, decentralization has forced specialization. Congress in committees deals with so many issues simultaneously that it is impossible for members to keep up

with much that goes on outside of their respective committees. Therefore the body usually chooses to (is forced to) rely upon the committees and subcommittees to produce legislation in each respective
field. This would be acceptable if each committee and subcommittee
was representative of the body as a whole. While this is rarely the case,
because congresspeople seek out places on committees that can help
their constituents, I believe that the creation of a committee dealing
with foreign affairs that reflects the body as a whole is also *impossible*
because too many interests come into play on different issues in the
foreign policy arena. In the case of the Agriculture Committee, there
are basically two interests that need to be represented: producer and
consumer. For a foreign affairs committee, however, there are myriads
of interests that need to be represented (for example, ethnic groups
with interests in their respective lands of origin, different businesses
interested in investing in different overseas nations, businesses afraid
of foreign competition, consumers of imported goods, all exporters,
and others).

Another barrier to rational policy-making that arises out of the
committee system is that foreign policy jurisdiction is spread out
among different committees. In the House, jurisdiction over foreign
intelligence belongs to the Armed Services Committee. However, CIA
covert operations are now primarily overseen by the Permanent Select
Committee on Intelligence. Foreign commerce generally belongs to
the Committee on Interstate and Foreign Commerce, and the list
continues.

Thus the structure of Congress does not lend itself to flexibility,
speed, or rationality.

A CHANGE IN ATTITUDE OCCURS

The change in Congress's attitude toward giving the president a
fairly free hand in the foreign policy arena can be seen in the following two quotes:

> I wonder whether the time has not arrived, or indeed already passed,
> when we must give the Executive a measure of power in the conduct of
> world affairs that we [the congresspeople] have hitherto jealously with-
> held. . . . It is my contention that for the existing requirements of Amer-
> ican foreign policy we have hobbled the President by too niggardly a
> grant of power.[15]

> Only if one subscribes to the cult of the "strong" Presidency which
> mesmerized American political science in the '50's and early '60's can
> one look with complacency on the growth of Presidential dictatorship

in foreign affairs. In those days, when the magic glow of Roosevelt still flickered in our memories, when Eisenhower resigned with paternal benignancy and the Kennedys appeared on white chargers with promises of Camelot, it was possible to forget the wisdom of the Founding Fathers, who had taught us to mistrust power, to check it and balance it, and never to yield up the means of thwarting it. Now, after bitter experience, we are having to learn all over again what those pre-Freudian students of human nature who framed the American Constitution understood well; that no single man or institution can ever be counted upon as a reliable or predictable repository of wisdom or benevolence; that the possession of great power can impair a man's judgment and cloud his perception of realities; and that our only protection against misuse of power is the institutionalized interaction of a diversity of politically independent opinion. . . . I believe that the Presidency has become a dangerously powerful office, more urgently in need for reform than any other institution in American government. . . . Whatever may be said against Congress—that it is slow, obstreperous, ineffecient or behind the times—there is one thing to be said for it: It poses no threat to the liberties of the American people.[16]

The reason that these two quotes represent Congress's change in attitude toward presidential power in foreign affairs so well is that both of them were stated by the same person. Senator Fulbright espoused the former position in 1961, only to come out with the latter in 1974. During these years, the Vietnam War and President Nixon's foreign policy power plays in Laos, Cambodia, and elsewhere so upset Congress that Congress "revolted" and seized many of the foreign policy powers that had previously been left to the president. Before attempting to state what should be done, let us clarify what the present situation is.

HOW MUCH POWER DOES CONGRESS HAVE OVER EXECUTIVE AGREEMENTS?

Between 1969 and 1972, three resolutions aimed at limiting or clarifying the use of executive agreements were passed by the Senate:

1. The national commitments resolution, S. Res. 85 (91st Congress), which was passed on June 25, 1969, expressed the sense of the Senate that a U.S. national commitment should result "only from affirmative action taken by the executive and legislative branches of the United States Government by means of a treaty, statute, or concurrent resolution of both Houses of Congress specifically providing for such commitment." According to the resolution, a na-

tional commitment was "the use of U.S. armed forces on foreign territory or a promise to assist a foreign country, government, or people by the use of U.S. armed forces or financial resources."

2. The resolution on the Spanish Bases Agreement, S. Res. 469 (91st Congress), was passed in December, 1970, expressing the sense of the Senate that nothing in the executive agreement with Spain should be deemed to be a national commitment by the United States. (The 1970 agreement extended the original 1953 agreement covering American use of bases in Spain.)

3. In March 1972 the Senate passed S. Res. 214 (92nd Congress), resolving that "any agreement with Portugal or Bahrain for military bases or foreign assistance should be submitted as a treaty to the Senate for advice and consent.[17]

In August 1972, the Congress passed the Case-Zablocki Act, which requires that any international agreement other than a treaty be transmitted to Congress no later than 60 days after the agreement enters into force (P.L. 92-403). Special procedures were set up for agreements whose sensitive nature called for secrecy.

As is often the case, things did not run as smoothly as had been intended. A February 1976 General Accounting Office report examined the implementation of the Case-Zablocki Act with respect to U.S. agreements with the Republic of Korea. The GAO identified 34 agreements that had been made after the passage of the Act (August 22, 1972) and that had not been transmitted to Congress. The problem was that these agreements had been made by agencies other than the State Department and had never been submitted to the State Department. To ameliorate this situation, Congress amended the Case-Zablocki Act in the Department of State supplemental appropriation for fiscal year 1977 (section 5) to require that "any department or agency of the United States Government which enters into any international agreement on behalf of the United States shall transmit to the Department of State the text of such agreement not later than twenty days after such agreement has been signed." This amendment sought to ensure that the State Department, which is required by law to transmit all executive agreements to Congress, has copies of all such agreements.[18]

The Case-Zablocki Act was amended further in 1978. These amendments

1. require the transmittal of oral international agreements which shall be reduced to writing;

2. require the President to report annually on the agreements which were transmitted late, describing "fully and completely" the reasons for the late transmittal;
3. stipulate that no agreement shall be signed or concluded without prior consultation with the Secretary of State or President;
4. identify the Secretary of State as the officer who shall determine "for and within the executive branch" whether an agreement constitutes an international agreement under the Act;
5. authorize the President, through the Secretary of State, to promulgate rules and regulations necessary to carry out the Act.[19]

In five acts, outlined below, Congress included provisions whereby executive agreements are to be submitted to the Congress *before* they go into force. These agreements are to enter into force within a certain period of time unless Congress moves to prevent this.

1. The Atomic Energy Act of 1954, as amended by the Nuclear Non-Proliferation Act of 1978 (P.L. 95-242), authorizes the President to conclude international agreements for U.S. cooperation with other nations in the transfer of nuclear technology and materials. It requires that such agreements be submitted to Congress for a period of 60 days and that, if a concurrent resolution stating that the Congress does not favor the proposed agreement is passed within such time, the agreement will not enter into force. The Act requires that the agreements be referred to the House International Relations and Senate Foreign Relations Committees and, in the case of agreements relating to military uses, to the House and Senate Committees on Armed Services.
2. The Trade Act of 1974 (P.L. 93-618) establishes procedures for congressional review of the exercise of presidential power in the foreign trade area. With regard to certain agreements, the President is authorized to conclude and implement trade agreements which lower nontariff barriers (Sec. 101) but these agreements are to enter into force for the United States only if, after transmittal to Congress of the text of the agreement, the implementing bill, and a statement of administrative action proposed, the Congress enacts the implementing bill, which, among other ingredients, includes a provision approving the trade agreement (Sec. 102 (e), Sec. 151). In addition, commercial agreements which grant nondiscriminatory tariff treatment to communist countries are to enter into force for the United States only after the Congress, by concurrent resolution, approves them. (Sec. 405 (c), Sec. 151.)

3. Under Title II of the Fishery Conservation and Management Act of 1976 (P.L. 94-265), no international fishery agreement entered into pursuant to section 201 (c) of the Act shall be effective for the United States until the end of 60 days after its transmittal by the President to the House and Senate. The Act also provided that within that 60-day period a joint resolution could be passed prohibiting its entering into force.

4. The Social Security Amendments of 1977 (P.L. 95-216, approved Dec. 20, 1977), Section 317—international agreements with respect to social security benefits—authorizes the President to enter into agreements establishing totalization arrangements between the U.S. social security system and that of any foreign country, for the purposes of establishing entitlement to and the amount of old-age, survivors, disability, or derivative benefits based on a combination of an individual's periods of coverage under the two systems. Any such agreement shall be transmitted to Congress, and if, during 90 days after such submission, either house adopts a resolution of disapproval of the agreement, the agreement will not enter into force.

5. The Foreign Disaster Assistance Act of 1974 (P.L. 93-333, approved July 8, 1974), requires the Secretary of State to keep the appropriate committees of Congress fully and currently informed of the status of any negotiations with any foreign government regarding the cancellation, renegotiation, rescheduling, or settlement of any debt owed to the United States by any such foreign government under the Foreign Assistance Act of 1961. Any agreement proposing a modification in the terms of such debt shall be transmitted to the Congress no less than 30 days prior to its entry into force, together with a detailed explanation of the U.S. interest in such modification. This Act does not include a provision for congressional disapproval of such agreements.[20]

Chart 3 illustrates the differences between these acts, differences which members of the executive branch must remember if they are to follow the law. (The War Powers Act will be discussed in detail later in this chapter.)

This chart demonstrates the confusion that members of the executive branch must deal with when they make executive agreements. Some agreements go into effect unless Congress disapproves (with a time limit that varies from act to act), while others do not go into force unless Congress approves. Some can be canceled by concurrent

Chart 3 Limitations on Executive Agreements Pursuant to Five Public Laws

Actions Limiting Use of Executive Agreements	Status of any Agreement	Time Limit	Joint or Concurrent Resolution or Bill Passed
Atomic Energy Act of 1954	Not in force if Congress says no within 60 days. Otherwise goes into effect.	60 days	Concurrent resolution
Trade Act of 1974	Not in force until Congress enacts implementing bill.		Concurrent resolution needed only for communist nations
Fishery Act of 1976	In effect unless Congress disapproves.	60 days	Joint resolution
War Powers Act	In effect for 90 days (60 in, 30 to leave) no matter what Congress does.	90 days	Canceled only congressional inaction (automatically)
Social Security Amendments	Not in force if Congress says no within 90 days. Otherwise goes into effect.	90 days	Resolution by either house cancels agreement

resolution, others by a resolution from either house, and still others are canceled automatically if Congress does not act. There may or may not be a rational reason for the lack of uniformity within these laws, but there is certainly confusion within the executive branch when its members rush to learn which set of rules must be followed for a given agreement.

THE WAR POWERS ACT

The most famous, and quite possibly the most important, attempt by Congress to restrict the president in foreign policy is the War Powers Resolution (Public Law 93-148). Adopted on November 7, 1973, this joint resolution seeks to limit the president's ability to commit U.S. troops to a potentially conflictual situation, the most dangerous executive agreement of them all.

The main points of the War Powers Resolution are that:

1. the president shall consult with Congress before introducing troops into a potentially conflictual situation "in every possible instance;"
2. once troops have been committed the president must submit a report to Congress within 48 hours outlining why the military was introduced into the situation, the constitutional and legislative authority upon which the introduction was based, and the "estimated scope and duration of the hostilities."[2][1]
3. After the report has been submitted, the president has 60 days for completion of the military action, and 30 additional days to withdraw the troops. The troops may stay longer only if (a) Congress has declared war, (b) Congress has extended the sixty-day period by law, or (c) Congress is unable to meet due to an armed attack upon the United States.[2][2]

This resolution has many interesting points. Constitutional scholars can argue that Congress is relinquishing some of its power because the Constitution states that only Congress can declare war, while the War Powers Resolution gives the president *90 days* during which he can commit troops to combat and quite conceivably cause another nation to declare war on the United States. The fact that this resolution was passed to *limit* presidential power shows how far practice is from what the theory (in the Constitution) was.

The passage of the War Powers Resolution represents (in my opinion) an admission by Congress of its own weaknesses. If Congress thought that it could act in a concerted, efficient manner whenever it needed to, and if Congress controlled the purse to the degree that it is supposed to, then Congress would know that it could end a U.S. troop involvement whenever it so desired simply by cutting off funds. By passing the War Powers Resolution, Congress is telling the president that if the Constitution is not clear enough with respect to congressional input in the war-making process, then here is a resolution that is. If a president ignores so clear a resolution, there exist clear grounds for impeachment.

Impeachment, however, is never undertaken lightly. It is probable that a large number of U.S. troops would have to be involved in a very unpopular military action for a long period of time before impeachment would even be considered. Due to its harshness, impeachment does not seem to be Congress's best tool for enforcing the War Powers Resolution, for presidents know how rarely this action is taken. If

Congress is going to enforce this resolution, then control of the purse must be regained.

PROS OF CONGRESSIONAL INVOLVEMENT IN FOREIGN POLICY

Despite all of the aforementioned "cons" that make Congress a poor partner for the president in the foreign policy process, there are numerous benefits to be had from congressional participation. Open debate educates the public and legitimizes our international commitments. More importantly, "rule by one is incompatible with American constitutional government."[2][3]

WHAT, THEN, IS THE ANSWER?

What, then, is the answer? How can the United States have the efficiency of rule by a philosopher-king along with the safety of a democracy?

Both Robert Dahl and George Grassmuck saw party discipline as the answer. If both the presidential and congressional candidates had to carry out the party platform if elected, then the voters could hold the majority party's representatives responsible for the actions of the government. (To a large degree this is done now, even though the parties themselves cannot discipline their candidates very well in the United States.) To be able to control (discipline) their president and congresspeople, parties would have to be given control over the selection process for candidates and all funds.

Simply to institute party discipline without altering the political system would be disastrous. What occurs if the party that controls Congress differs from the party of the president? Such a relationship existed during the Ford administration. Stalemate and inaction were often the result. Clearly, even if one party has enough votes in both houses to override vetoes, the Constitution has placed the power to initiate foreign policy actions in the hands of the president.

If we were to change the system to one similar to the British, party discipline could create a more consistent foreign policy-making machine. The British system does an excellent job of allowing the party leaders to have some flexibility even as they are held relatively responsible. Like every other system, however, it has its flaws. No modern British prime minister has ever lost a vote of confidence. Even Neville Chamberlain was not "booted out" after the Munich debacle, which quickly became a very, very unpopular decision. His majority shrank, but it did not disappear because party discipline was so strong. This demonstrates that the executive is only held relatively responsible. The degree of responsibility is still unclear and probably varies from nation to nation, and even from prime minister to prime minister. In 1956 Anthony Eden may have been forced out by his party's members of Parliament, but it is not clear that this was the case. The British system offers one example to be considered.

Since it is unlikely that the United States will change to a Parliamentary system of government in the forseeable future, what is an alternative solution? How can the United States have flexibility *and* responsibility in foreign policy decision making?

It is a mistake for Congress to try to be the president's equal in the making of executive agreements and in the foreign policy arena in general. In my opinion, Congress goes too far when it insists upon the right to approve or disapprove executive agreements *before* they go into effect. This not only greatly inhibits the president's flexibility in foreign policy, but it magnifies the problems that go with congressional participation, such as a lack of secrecy, slowness of action, and so forth.

The answer probably lies in proper oversight by Congress of executive foreign policy initiatives. Congress has always controlled the purse, which makes it the dominant institution in every field that it chooses to dominate. Excessive congressional interference in the foreign policy arena is unlikely because most citizens grossly underestimate the effect of foreign policy actions on their lives. Since so many constituents care less about foreign than domestic policy, it is not worth much in political capital for congresspeople. In time they lose interest in foreign policy concerns, only to be reminded of their oversight duties when presidents overstep their boundaries. While Congress is presently quite wary of presidential actions in foreign policy, it is only a matter of time before laxity is again the case. Congress ought not to be a partner in the foreign policy decision-making process, but constant oversight by the legislature is a must in a democracy. The key is the purse. Earlier in this study we noted that Congress has been careless in guarding its control over this, its most important resource. Rather than have Congress codetermine foreign policy (have a major input into the decision-making process), let Congress *investigate* the CIA, armed forces, and so forth, as it investigates the bureaucracy, and punish these organs as it punishes the bureaucracy, by cutting off funds. In this manner the executive will be allowed to initiate responses or policies at first, but will know (and the heads of all of the foreign policy organs will know) that if the will of Congress is ignored, then punishment will be severe. To avoid punishment, or even destruction, the foreign policy organs and the president will soon learn that they should consult Congress *before* they act. They will not, however, have to wait for Congress to pass legislation before taking action. Legislative oversight, a Samuel Huntington solution, allows for presidential flexibility while providing the safeguards of democracy. Perhaps in foreign policy we do need an elected monarch, but the regent's philosophy for action must be shaped with help from Congress.

NOTES

1. Alexander Hamilton, James Madison, and John Jay, *The Federalist*, Number 75, in *The Federalist Papers*, intro. Clinton Rossiter (New York: The New American Library, Mentor Book, 1971), pp. 452-53.

2. George Grassmuck, *Sectional Biases in Congress on Foreign Policy* (Baltimore: Johns Hopkins Press, 1951), p. 162.

3. Alexander DeConde, ed., *A History of American Foreign Policy* (New York: Charles Scribner's Sons, 1978), 2:127 and 2:262.

4. Thomas M. Franck and Edward Weisband, *Foreign Policy by Congress* (Oxford: Oxford University Press, 1979), pp. 191-92.

5. Ibid., pp. 51-53.

6. Ibid., p. 165.

7. Ibid., p. 103.

8. Ibid.

9. Ibid., p. 120.

10. Ibid., p. 126.

11. Ibid., p. 130.

12. Ibid., p. 5.

13. Ibid., p. 29.

14. Robert Dahl, *Congress and Foreign Policy* (New York: Harcourt, Brace, & Company, 1950), p. 125.

15. Franck and Weisband, *Foreign Policy by Congress*, p. 4.

16. Ibid., pp. 4-5.

17. Marjorie Ann Browne, "Executive Agreements and the Congress," The Library of Congress Congressional Research Service Major Issues System, Issue Brief Number IB75035, originated May 1, 1975, updated February 27, 1981, p. 3.

18. Ibid., p. 5.

19. Ibid.

20. Ibid., p. 6.

21. The War Powers Resolution, Public Law 93-148, Section 4.

22. Ibid., Section 5.

23. Grassmuck, *Sectional Biases in Congress on Foreign Policy*, p. 11.

8

AN ANSWER?

Up until the twentieth century, U.S. presidents averaged approximately one executive agreement per year. Very few of these agreements had any national significance, and those that did often caused an uproar. Important matters were supposed to be settled by treaties according to most citizens' interpretations of the Constitution. While the Constitution does say that states can make agreements with foreign nations, but not treaties, which suggests that the Constitution does recognize that nontreaty agreements exist, nowhere in the Constitution is it said that the president can make such agreements. In addition the Constitution says that these agreements made by the states must be approved by Congress. Therefore, I doubt that many of the Founding Fathers would have considered executive agreements to be constitutional when first confronted with this phenomenon. However, a more in-depth study of the situation might have caused them to favor executive agreements and to adopt the broadest possible interpretation of the Constitution so as to allow for their continuation.

It would only take these Founding Fathers a few minutes to realize how much the world has changed in two centuries. Improved communications and transportation make the world seem much smaller, and we must deal with other nations (and a much larger number of nations) frequently instead of very rarely. This has greatly increased the number of agreements that must be made. It used to take weeks or even months before the United States of America could even know it was confronted by a nation in Europe that had declared war. Now we can be decimated within minutes.

The Founding Fathers would also see that the United States is now the world's strongest nation, and that the United States' greatly increased involvement in world affairs increases the number of agreements that must be made.

With so many more agreements needing to be made, the treaty process, with its slow and deliberate manner, might not seem adequate. Sometimes over 300 executive agreements are concluded in a year. Could the Senate pass a treaty per day? Those who know the Senate well probably have serious doubts that this could be done. Could 100 Senators (and 435 Representatives, when the treaty came up for funding) keep something a secret? This also seems unlikely. Enthusiasts of open government would welcome the end of executive agreements. They would argue that the United States should have nothing to hide. Idealistically, this should be true, but in reality secrecy is a vital part of government. Beyond the obvious need for secrecy with respect to military and intelligence matters, there is still a vital need for secrecy in foreign policy. Secrecy greatly increases a leader's flexibility in that the heads of other governments are often willing to agree to certain things *if* they can be kept secret from their followers. Envoys from the United States government have most probably been talking to various leaders of the Palestine Liberation Organization for years. Since our ally Israel does not care for this, and the lower-level PLO members might choose to change leaders if they knew of this, secrecy is imperative. Therefore, I doubt that any agreements between the United States and the PLO could conceivably be worked out if they had to go through the treaty process.

While secrecy helps certain individuals to survive, politically if not literally, it also helps others to "save face." Earlier we noted that the leaders of the Soviet Union were willing to ease emigration barriers for Soviet Jews only to change their minds as senators kept openly pushing for more. It was not what the senators were requesting that caused them to cut off the deal; it was the way in which the senators were bullying the USSR for everyone to see. This the Soviets could not accept.

Besides the benefits of speed and secrecy, the use of executive agreements is even more inviting because the overwhelming majority of them are still used to resolve relatively routine matters. Few congresspeople would ever object to a postal agreement, or to an agreement that allows other nations to use our air space for commercial flights if we can use theirs. Congresspeople do not want to waste their time on such things. Appendix B lists most of the executive agreements made by President Carter with Mexico and Egypt, the two nations with which most executive agreements were made, during his second year in office (January 20, 1978-January 20, 1979). Many of the agreements with Mexico dealt with stopping the drug traffic between the two nations. Congress certainly would not object to these, and it is doubtful that Congress as a whole would object strongly, if at all, to any of the agreements made with Mexico and Egypt during that year.

It is very difficult to estimate what percentage of executive agreements are attempts by the president to avoid having to pass a treaty through the Senate. The State Department has stated that at least 90 percent of all executive agreements follow the will of Congress. The State Department was simply taking its best, and possibly biased, guess. I do not share in the State Department's interest, but I would guess that their estimate is a pretty good one. The overwhelming majority of executive agreements would receive little opposition from Congress. Many executive agreements are made after Congress has called for them to be concluded.

Quantity, however, is not the only issue. Those relatively rare occasions when presidents do use executive agreements just to avoid the Senate and its treaty process are often, as one might suspect, very significant agreements. Appendix C contains the verbiage of two agreements. One is typically noncontroversial, while the other helped to get the United States into World War II by giving Britain fifty destroyers in exchange for bases in the Caribbean.

When presidents do seek to avoid the Senate, it is not necessarily because they are "evil" or power hungry. Different people have different visions of the United States and what its goals should be. Most historians agree today that President Roosevelt was wise in trying to get the United States into World War II before Germany and Japan had acquired too strong a position. In addition, presidents are aware of the strength that interest groups exercise in Congress, and the fact that only the president is elected by the entire nation. This fact, and their access to more information, from the CIA and State Department, may cause presidents to believe that they "know better" than Congress.

Indeed, this work has shown that even the political party affiliation of the president has very little effect on the types of agreements that are made. Democrats and Republicans keep our foreign policy on more or less the same path. They agree on the direction that our nation should follow.

With all of the reasons and experience that have been discussed, we could probably convince most of our Founding Fathers that executive agreements are at least a necessary evil, if not a positive good. However, few, if any, of these men would want to exclude Congress from the foreign policy process by giving it no say on these agreements. We fought a revolution against tyranny, and as Plato pointed out, the chances for tyranny are greatest when power is concentrated in the hands of one person. When presidents use executive agreements to avoid the Senate, and fund them without asking for an appropriation from Congress, then we are in that instance close to tyranny. This situation is not acceptable, no matter how rare the cases are.

After World War II and the United States' emergence as a world power, congresspeople realized that there was a much greater need for speed, flexibility, and secrecy in foreign policy than there ever had been before. In addition it seemed to most that the Soviet Union was a threat to security, so there would be little difference between what Democratic presidents would have to do as opposed to their Republican counterparts. A bipartisan approach to foreign policy came into being, and it has remained to this day.

All of the aforementioned reasons caused Congress to grant presidents greater flexibility in foreign policy. For example, Congress was once content to know how much money was spent by the Central Intelligence Agency, but not how any of it was spent. Section 614 of the Foreign Assistance Act (discussed earlier) authorized the president to give up to $250 million to any country that is "a victim of active Communist or Communist supported aggression." Congress saw how the world had changed, realized that the president was better equipped to deal with these changes, and responded by yielding large amounts of power to the president.

After the United States' involvement in the undeclared war in Vietnam, achieved by a series of executive agreements and one joint resolution, many citizens called for Congress to regain its rightful position as the president's partner in foreign policy decision making. For all of the reasons outlined in the previous chapter, I could not disagree more. Congress was wise to grant the president greater leeway in foreign policy. Where it was unwise was in letting the executive get *total control* in many instances where some control is really necessary.

When Congress truly controlled the funding process, it did not matter that presidents were using executive agreements to circumvent the Senate. Very little could be done without money, and only Congress could provide this commodity. However, Congress was not vigilant in preserving its monopoly. It willingly yielded large sums of money to the president to be spent at executive discretion. It also failed to realize that large sums of money were being accumulated by members of the executive branch in a wide variety of ways. Congress, once the proud possessor of the ultimate power, suddenly found itself powerless in many instances. Weapons were manufactured, programs were initiated, and wars were waged without Congress even voting a penny towards these actions. To regain control of the purse, the General Accounting Office staff may have to be increased. A more watchful eye should ensure that bureaucratic agencies return unspent capital. The amount of hidden money has to be greatly decreased. Congress has been lax in guarding its control over the purse. This must cease.

The Constitution never meant for Congress to be an equal in the foreign policy process. It was the president who was given the power to negotiate treaties (decide what they would say). Congress could only approve or disapprove of the final form. If Congress can regain control of the purse, the same situation would exist, only in a different form. The president and the other members of the executive branch would be able to make executive agreements quickly and with secrecy, but these agreements would not really be in effect until Congress appropriated the funds for them. Presidents would not be able to siphon off money from other funds if Congress tightly controlled the purse. Congress must not, however, do what it has done so many times in the past and forget about foreign policy. Congress must be vigilant at all times.

Few solutions are perfect. This one certainly is not. Presidents would make agreements, and a few months later Congress would refuse to provide funding for them. At first, U.S. foreign policy might seem even more inconsistent that it currently does. However, presidents would quickly learn that they should consult key congresspeople while negotiating executive agreements so that they would be aware of Congress's wishes. With all of its imperfections, this solution seems to allow for speed and secrecy without sacrificing democracy.

APPENDIXES

A. TABLES

Table 1   Number of Executive Agreements and Treaties Made in Each Presidential Year

President	Year of Term	Party of President	Senate Majority Party (Same or Different than President's)	Number of Agreements	Number of Treaties
Washington	1	Admin.	same	0	0
Washington	2	Admin.	same	0	0
Washington	3	Federalists	same	0	0
Washington	4	Federalists	same	0	0
Washington	5	Federalists	same	0	0
Washington	6	Federalists	same	0	1
Washington	7	Federalists	same	0	2
Washington	8	Federalists	same	0	2
Adams	1	Federalists	same	0	1
Adams	2	Federalists	same	0	1
Adams	3	Federalists	same	0	1
Adams	4	Federalists	same	0	1
Jefferson	1	Dem-Rep	same	0	1
Jefferson	2	Dem-Rep	same	0	1
Jefferson	3	Dem-Rep	same	0	3
Jefferson	4	Dem-Rep	same	0	0
Jefferson	5	Dem-Rep	same	0	1
Jefferson	6	Dem-Rep	same	0	0
Jefferson	7	Dem-Rep	same	0	0
Jefferson	8	Dem-Rep	same	0	0
Madison	1	Dem-Rep	same	0	0
Madison	2	Dem-Rep	same	0	0
Madison	3	Dem-Rep	same	0	0
Madison	4	Dem-Rep	same	0	0
Madison	5	Dem-Rep	same	0	0
Madison	6	Dem-Rep	same	0	1
Madison	7	Dem-Rep	same	0	2
Madison	8	Dem-Rep	same	0	2
Monroe	1	Dem-Rep	same	1	0
Monroe	2	Dem-Rep	same	0	2
Monroe	3	Dem-Rep	same	0	0
Monroe	4	Dem-Rep	same	0	0
Monroe	5	Dem-Rep	same	0	0
Monroe	6	Dem-Rep	same	0	2
Monroe	7	Dem-Rep	same	0	1
Monroe	8	Dem-Rep	same	0	2
J. Q. Adams	1	Admin.	same	1	1
J. Q. Adams	2	Admin.	same	1	2
J. Q. Adams	3	Jacksonians	diff.	0	6
J. Q. Adams	4	Jacksonians	diff.	0	3

Table 1–*continues*

101

Table 1—*continued*

President	Year of Term	Party of President	Senate Majority Party (Same or Different than President's)	Number of Agreements	Number of Treaties
Jackson	1	Democrats	same	0	1
Jackson	2	Democrats	same	0	2
Jackson	3	Democrats	same	0	2
Jackson	4	Democrats	same	0	3
Jackson	5	Democrats	same	0	4
Jackson	6	Democrats	same	0	0
Jackson	7	Democrats	same	0	2
Jackson	8	Democrats	same	0	2
Van Buren	1	Democrats	same	0	1
Van Buren	2	Democrats	same	0	4
Van Buren	3	Democrats	same	1	2
Van Buren	4	Democrats	same	1	2
W. H. Harrison (3/4-4/4/1841)	1	Whigs	same	0 (0)*	1 (12)
Tyler (4/6/1841 -3/4/1842)	1	Whigs	same	0 (0)	0 (0)
Tyler	2	Whigs	same	0	2
Tyler	3	Whigs	same	1	2
Tyler	4	Whigs	same	0	6
Polk	1	Democrats	same	1	3
Polk	2	Democrats	same	2	4
Polk	3	Democrats	same	1	5
Polk	4	Democrats	same	1	4
Taylor	1	Whigs	diff.	3	2
Taylor (3/6-7/9/1850)	2	Whigs	diff.	0 (0)	2 (6)
Fillmore (7/10/1850- 3/4/1851)	1	Whigs	diff.	1 (1.5)	2 (3)
Fillmore	2	Whigs	diff.	0	2
Fillmore	3	Whigs	diff.	3	5
Pierce	1	Democrats	same	5	5
Pierce	2	Democrats	same	4	9
Pierce	3	Democrats	same	3	1
Pierce	4	Democrats	same	0	5
Buchanan	1	Democrats	same	3	5
Buchanan	2	Democrats	same	1	9
Buchanan	3	Democrats	same	2	0
Buchanan	4	Democrats	same	2	2
Lincoln	1	Republicans	same	0	8
Lincoln	2	Republicans	same	1	6
Lincoln	3	Republicans	same	2	5
Lincoln	4	Republicans	same	0	3
Lincoln (3/4-4/15/1865)	5	Republicans	same	0 (0)	0 (0)

Table 1—*continues*

Table 1—*continued*

President	Year of Term	Party of President	Senate Majority Party (Same or Different than President's)	Number of Agreements	Number of Treaties
Johnson (4/15/1865- 3/4/1866)	1	Republicans	same	0 (0)	0 (0)
Johnson	2	Republicans	same	0	5
Johnson	3	Republicans	same	0	7
Johnson	4	Republicans	same	0	14
Grant	1	Republicans	same	1	2
Grant	2	Republicans	same	1	11
Grant	3	Republicans	same	0	5
Grant	4	Republicans	same	0	5
Grant	5	Republicans	same	2	2
Grant	6	Republicans	same	5	4
Grant	7	Republicans	same	0	1
Grant	8	Republicans	same	2	2
Hayes	1	Republicans	same	1	1
Hayes	2	Republicans	same	1	5
Hayes	3	Republicans	diff.	1	1
Hayes	4	Republicans	diff.	2	7
Garfield (3/4-9/19/1881)	1	Republicans	same	1 (2)	2 (4)
Arthur (9/20/1881- 3/4/1882)	1	Republicans	same	0 (0)	2 (4)
Arthur	2	Republicans	same	4	10
Arthur	3	Republicans	same	4	2
Arthur	4	Republicans	same	3	8
Cleveland	1	Democrats	diff.	5	2
Cleveland	2	Democrats	diff.	1	7
Cleveland	3	Democrats	diff.	3	4
Cleveland	4	Democrats	diff.	2	6
Harrison	1	Republicans	same	1	2
Harrison	2	Republicans	same	2	2
Harrison	3	Republicans	same	6	5
Harrison	4	Republicans	same	2	7
Cleveland	5	Democrats	same	0	2
Cleveland	6	Democrats	same	2	3
Cleveland	7	Democrats	diff.	2	2
Cleveland	8	Democrats	diff.	2	4
McKinley	1	Republicans	same	2	3
McKinley	2	Republicans	same	7	4
McKinley	3	Republicans	same	9	9
McKinley	4	Republicans	same	7	8
McKinley (3/4-9/14/1901)	5	Republicans	same	2 (4)	2 (4)

Table 1—*continues*

Table 1—*continued*

President	Year of Term	Party of President	Senate Majority Party (Same or Different than President's)	Number of Agreements	Number of Treaties
T. Roosevelt (9/14/1901- 3/4/1902)	1	Republicans	same	4 (8)	7 (14)
T. Roosevelt	2	Republicans	same	9	11
T. Roosevelt	3	Republicans	same	1	11
T. Roosevelt	4	Republicans	same	7	13
T. Roosevelt	5	Republicans	same	10	7
T. Roosevelt	6	Republicans	same	7	13
T. Roosevelt	7	Republicans	same	10	15
T. Roosevelt	8	Republicans	same	4	35
Taft	1	Republicans	same	7	4
Taft	2	Republicans	same	5	12
Taft	3	Republicans	same	2	8
Taft	4	Republicans	same	3	4
Wilson	1	Democrats	same	4	15
Wilson	2	Democrats	same	7	23
Wilson	3	Democrats	same	13	1
Wilson	4	Democrats	same	7	2
Wilson	5	Democrats	same	4	1
Wilson	6	Democrats	same	9	12
Wilson	7	Democrats	diff.	7	11
Wilson	8	Democrats	diff.	3	3
Harding	1	Republicans	same	14	13
Harding	2	Republicans	same	10	8
Harding (3/4-8/2/1923)	3	Republicans	same	7 (16.8)	7 (16.8)
Coolidge (8/3/1923- 3/4/1924)	1	Republicans	same	6 (10.3)	13 (22.3)
Coolidge	2	Republicans	same	18	28
Coolidge	3	Republicans	same	38	13
Coolidge	4	Republicans	same	21	7
Coolidge	5	Republicans	same	14	10
Coolidge	6	Republicans	same	23	41
Hoover	1	Republicans	same	26	21
Hoover	2	Republicans	same	19	17
Hoover	3	Republicans	same	22	7
Hoover	4	Republicans	same	38	8
F. Roosevelt	1	Democrats	same	19	7
F. Roosevelt	2	Democrats	same	21	16
F. Roosevelt	3	Democrats	same	21	11
F. Roosevelt	4	Democrats	same	26	25
F. Roosevelt	5	Democrats	same	23	13
F. Roosevelt	6	Democrats	same	38	9
F. Roosevelt	7	Democrats	same	30	10

Table 1—*continues*

Table 1—*continued*

President	Year of Term	Party of President	Senate Majority Party (Same or Different than President's)	Number of Agreements	Number of Treaties
F. Roosevelt	8	Democrats	same	29	13
F. Roosevelt	9	Democrats	same	56	4
F. Roosevelt	10	Democrats	same	130	4
F. Roosevelt	11	Democrats	same	98	1
F. Roosevelt	12	Democrats	same	83	6
F. Roosevelt (1/20-4/12/1945)	13	Democrats	same	35 (140)	0 (0)
Truman (4/12/1945-1/20/1946)	1	Democrats	same	85 (113.3)	5 (6.7)
Truman	2	Democrats	same	144	19
Truman	3	Democrats	diff.	174	18
Truman	4	Democrats	diff.	202	21
Truman	5	Democrats	same	200	36
Truman	6	Democrats	same	156	17
Truman	7	Democrats	same	246	17
Truman	8	Democrats	same	259	11
Eisenhower	1	Republicans	same	160	17
Eisenhower	2	Republicans	same	203	15
Eisenhower	3	Republicans	diff.	314	7
Eisenhower	4	Republicans	diff.	237	16
Eisenhower	5	Republicans	diff.	209	7
Eisenhower	6	Republicans	diff.	196	14
Eisenhower	7	Republicans	diff.	238	8
Eisenhower	8	Republicans	diff.	267	7
Kennedy	1	Democrats	same	249	11
Kennedy	2	Democrats	same	320	10
Kennedy (1/20-11/22/1963)	3	Democrats	same	190 (228)	12 (14.4)
L. Johnson (11/22/1963-1/20/1964)	1	Democrats	same	29 (174)	1 (6)
L. Johnson	2	Democrats	same	220	4
L. Johnson	3	Democrats	same	212	14
L. Johnson	4	Democrats	same	225	13
L. Johnson	5	Democrats	same	223	13
L. Johnson	6	Democrats	same	180	6
Nixon	1	Republicans	diff.	159	12
Nixon	2	Republicans	diff.	211	15
Nixon	3	Republicans	diff.	219	17
Nixon	4	Republicans	diff.	276	19
Nixon	5	Republicans	diff.	224	11
Nixon (1/20-8/9/1974)	6	Republicans	diff.	145 (248.6)	5 (8.6)

Table 1—*continues*

Table 1—*continued*

President	Year of Term	Party of President	Senate Majority Party (Same or Different than President's)	Number of Agreements	Number of Treaties
Ford (8/9/1974- 1/20/1975)	1	Republicans	diff.	100 (240)	5 (12)
Ford	2	Republicans	diff.	291	7
Ford	3	Republicans	diff.	363	7
Carter	1	Democrats	same	371	4
Carter	2	Democrats	same	299	10

*The values in parentheses represent the number of agreements and treaties respectively that would have been made in a full year if the president had maintained the rate at which he made them during this abbreviated time period.

Table 1B Types of Agreements and Treaties Made by Modern Presidents

	Agreements						Treaties					
	Procedural		Goods		Military		Procedural		Goods		Military	
	No.	%	No.	%	No.	%	No.	%	No.	%	No.	%
Roosevelt												
1	18	94.7	1	5.3	0	0	7	87.5	0	0	1	12.5
2	17	80.9	1	4.8	3	14.3	12	85.7	2	14.3	0	
3	19	95.0	0		1	5.0	10	100.0	0		0	
4	22	84.6	1	3.8	3	11.5	19	76.0	1	4.0	5	20.0
5	22	95.7	1	4.3	0		10	90.9	1	9.1	0	
6	32	84.2	2	5.3	4	10.5	11	91.7	1	8.3	0	
7	23	76.7	0		7	23.3	8	88.9	1	11.1	0	
8	25	73.5	0		9	26.5	8	66.6	0		4	33.3
9	21	38.9	3	5.6	30	55.5	2	50.0	1	25.0	1	25.0
10	72	52.2	24	17.4	42	30.4	2	100.0	0		0	
11	41	43.6	20	21.3	33	35.1	3	100.0	0		0	
12	44	55.7	23	29.1	12	15.2	5	100.0	0		0	
13*	16	45.7	9	25.7	10	28.6	0		0		0	
Truman*												
1	47	49.5	18	18.9	30	31.6	6	100.0	0		0	
2	109	73.2	31	20.8	9	6.0	18	94.7	1	5.3	0	
3	108	60.3	54	30.2	17	9.5	15	75.0	0		5	25.0
4	112	55.2	81	39.9	10	4.9	16	84.2	2	10.5	1	5.3
5	106	55.2	68	35.4	18	9.4	36	97.3	0		1	2.7
6	61	37.4	69	42.3	33	20.2	14	100.0	0		0	
7	61	23.3	146	55.7	55	21.0	12	66.6	0		6	33.3
8	85	35.9	116	48.9	36	15.2	11	100.0	0		0	

Table 1B—*continues*

Table 1B—*continued*

	Agreements						Treaties					
	Procedural		Goods		Military		Procedural		Goods		Military	
	No.	%	No.	%	No.	%	No.	%	No.	%	No.	%
Eisenhower												
1	48	30.4	65	41.1	45	28.5	12	75.0	3	18.8	1	6.3
2	83	40.9	68	33.5	52	25.6	11	73.3	0		4	26.7
3	114	36.0	140	44.2	63	19.9	7	100.0	0		0	
4	88	37.0	106	44.5	44	18.5	16	100.0	0		0	
5	84	41.4	84	41.4	35	17.2	7	100.0	0		0	
6	65	33.5	93	47.9	36	18.6	13	100.0	0		0	
7	82	34.2	100	41.7	58	24.2	5	83.3	0		1	16.7
8	96	36.1	112	42.1	58	21.8	5	83.3	1	16.7	0	
Kennedy												
1	89	35.2	130	51.4	34	13.4	9	100.0	0		0	
2	112	35.9	161	51.6	39	12.5	10	100.0	0		0	
3*	97	52.2	77	41.4	12	6.5	11	100.0	0		0	
Johnson												
1	11	45.8	10	41.7	3	12.5	1	100.0	0		0	
2	113	50.4	94	42.0	17	7.6	4	100.0	0		0	
3	109	50.9	78	36.4	27	12.6	14	100.0	0		0	
4	112	49.8	94	41.8	19	8.4	14	100.0	0		0	
5	141	63.5	66	29.7	15	6.8	11	91.7	0		1	8.3
6	91	51.1	70	39.3	17	9.6	4	80.0	0		1	20.0
Nixon												
1	70	43.5	67	41.6	24	14.9	10	100.0	0		0	
2	123	58.6	65	31.0	22	10.5	15	100.0	0		0	
3	112	50.0	88	39.3	24	10.7	14	82.4	2	11.8	1	5.9
4	168	61.5	87	31.9	18	6.6	16	88.9	0		2	11.1
5	135	61.1	66	29.9	20	9.0	9	100.0	0		0	
6*	91	59.5	53	34.6	9	5.9	4	80.0	0		1	20.0
Ford												
1	66	61.1	36	33.3	6	5.6	4	100.0	0		0	
2	155	57.2	96	35.4	20	7.4	7	100.0	0		0	
3	185	49.7	166	44.6	21	5.6	6	100.0	0		0	
Carter												
1	189	52.4	159	44.0	13	3.6	3	100.0	0		0	
2	147	49.5	138	46.5	12	4.0	10	100.0	0		0	

*Indicates an abbreviated presidential year. Two consecutive years marked with an asterisk when combined equal one 365-day year.

Table 2 Number of Agreements and Treaties by Era

Era	Number of Agreements	Number of Treaties
1789-1800	0	8
1800-1900	115	312
1900-33	388	411
1933-79	8,405	550
Totals	8,908	1,281

Table 2B Agreements and Treaties Combined by Type for Each Presidential Year

President	Procedural		Goods		Military	
	No.	%	No.	%	No.	%
	Roosevelt					
1	25	92.6	1	3.7	1	3.7
2	29	82.9	3	8.6	3	8.6
3	29	96.7	0		1	3.3
4	41	80.4	2	3.9	8	15.7
5	32	94.1	2	5.9	0	
6	43	86.0	3	6.0	4	8.0
7	31	79.5	1	2.6	7	17.9
8	33	71.7	0		13	28.3
9	23	39.7	4	6.9	31	53.4
10	74	52.9	24	17.1	42	30.0
11	44	45.4	20	20.6	33	34.0
12	49	58.3	23	27.4	12	14.3
13*	16	45.7	9	25.7	10	28.6
	Truman*					
1	53	52.5	18	17.8	30	29.7
2	127	75.6	32	19.0	9	5.4
3	123	61.8	54	27.1	22	11.1
4	128	57.7	83	37.4	11	5.0
5	142	62.0	68	29.7	19	8.3
6	75	42.4	69	39.0	33	18.6
7	73	26.1	146	52.1	61	21.8
8	96	38.7	116	46.8	36	14.5
	Eisenhower					
1	60	34.5	68	39.1	46	26.4
2	94	43.1	68	31.2	56	25.7
3	121	37.3	140	43.2	63	19.4
4	104	40.9	106	41.7	44	17.3
5	91	43.3	84	40.0	35	16.7
6	78	37.8	93	44.9	36	17.4
7	87	35.4	100	40.6	59	24.0
8	101	37.1	113	41.5	58	21.3

Table 2B—*continues*

Table 2B—*continued*

President	Procedural No.	%	Goods No.	%	Military No.	%
	Kennedy					
1	98	37.4	130	49.6	34	13.0
2	122	37.9	161	50.0	39	12.1
3*	108	54.8	77	39.1	12	6.1
	Johnson*					
1	12	48.0	10	40.0	3	12.0
2	117	51.3	94	41.2	17	7.5
3	123	53.9	78	34.2	27	11.8
4	126	52.7	94	39.3	19	7.9
5	152	65.0	66	28.2	16	6.8
6	95	51.9	70	38.3	18	9.8
	Nixon					
1	80	46.8	67	39.2	24	14.0
2	138	61.3	65	28.9	22	9.8
3	126	52.3	90	37.3	25	10.4
4	184	63.2	87	29.9	20	6.9
5	144	62.6	66	28.7	20	8.7
6*	95	60.1	53	33.5	10	6.3
	Ford*					
1	70	62.5	36	32.1	6	5.4
2	162	58.3	96	34.5	20	7.2
3	191	50.5	166	43.9	21	5.6
	Carter					
1	192	52.7	159	43.7	13	3.6
2	157	51.1	138	45.0	12	3.9

*Indicates an abbreviated presidential year. Two consecutive years thus marked when combined equal one 365-day year.

Table 3 Percentage of Total Agreements and Treaties Made during Different Eras

Era	Agreements (percentage of the total made)	Treaties (percentage of the total made)
1789-1800	0	0.6
1800-1900	1.3	24.4
1900-33	4.4	32.1
1933-79	94.35	42.9

Table 3B Influence of Party on Types of Agreements and Treaties Concluded (in percent)

Type of Commitment	Roosevelt (D, 13 yrs.)	Truman (D, 8 yrs.)	Eisenhower (R, 8 yrs.)	Kennedy (D, 3 yrs.)	Johnson (D, 6 yrs.)	Nixon (R, 6 yrs.)	Ford (R, 3 yrs.)	Carter (D, 2 yrs.)
Procedural agreements and treaties	71.2	52.1	38.7	43.4	53.8	57.7	57.1	51.9
Agreements and treaties providing goods	9.9	33.6	40.3	46.2	36.9	32.9	36.8	44.4
Agreements and treaties related to military	18.9	14.3	21.0	10.4	9.3	9.4	6.1	3.8

Composite

	Democratic Presidents	Republican Presidents
Procedural agreements and treaties	54.5	51.2
Agreements and treaties providing goods	34.2	36.7
Agreements and treaties related to military	11.3	12.2

Table 4 Average Number of Agreements and Treaties Made per Year by Each Modern President

Roosevelt (D, 13 yrs.)	Truman (D, 8 yrs.)	Eisenhower (R, 8 yrs.)	Kennedy (D, 3 yrs.)	Johnson (D, 6 yrs.)	Nixon (R, 6 yrs.)	Ford (R, 3 yrs.)	Carter (D, 2 yrs.)
64.1	205.0	239.4	277.5	215.0	236.7	306.7	342.0

Table 5 Agreements per Treaty Ratio, When President and Senate Majority are of Same Party, and When They Are of a Different Party (each presidential year listed separately)

| | | | | | | Ratio | | | | | | |
| | | | | | | Year | | | | | | |
	1	2	3	4	5	6	7	8	9	10	11	12
President and Senate of the Same Party												
Roosevelt	2.7	1.3	1.9	1.0	1.8	4.2	3.0	2.2	14.0	32.5	98.0	13.8
FDR-Truman	24.0											
Truman		7.6			5.6	9.2	14.5	23.5				
Eisenhower	9.4	13.5										
Kennedy	22.6	32.0										
JFK-LBJ			16.8									
Johnson	55.0		15.1	17.3	17.2	30.0						
Carter	92.8	29.9										
President and Senate of Different Party												
Truman			9.6	9.6								
Eisenhower			44.8	14.8	29.8	14.0	29.8	38.1				
Nixon	13.3	14.1	12.9	14.5	20.4							
Nixon-Ford						24.5						
Ford		41.6	51.9									

Table 6 Effects of Running for Reelection on Average Number
of Agreements and Treaties Made

President	Average Number of Agreements and Treaties Made in Terms Where President Was Eligible for Reelection		
Franklin Roosevelt	*First term*		
	Average for the first 3 years	=	31.7
	Average for the 2nd and 3rd	=	34.5
	Fourth year	=	51.0
	Second term		
	Average for the first 3 years	=	41.0
	Average for the 2nd and 3rd	=	43.5
	Fourth year	=	42.0
	Third term		
	Average for the first 3 years	=	97.7
	Average for the 2nd and 3rd	=	116.5
	Fourth year	=	89.0
Harry Truman	*First term*		
	Average for the first 3 years (First year adjusted for shortened time period)	=	158.3
	Average for the 2nd and 3rd	=	177.5
	Fourth year	=	223.0
	Second term		
	Average for the first 3 years	=	224.0
	Average for the 2nd and 3rd	=	218.0
	Fourth year	=	270.0
Dwight Eisenhower	*First term*		
	Average for the first 3 years	=	238.7
	Average for the 2nd and 3rd	=	269.5
	Fourth year	=	253.0
Lyndon Johnson	*First elected term*		
	Average for the first 3 years	=	233.3
	Average for the 2nd and 3rd	=	237.0
	Fourth year	=	186.0
Richard Nixon	*First term*		
	Average for the first 3 years	=	211.0
	Average for the 2nd and 3rd	=	231.0
	Fourth year	=	295.0

Table 6B Effects of Elections on Types of Agreements and Treaties Made

President, Term, and Year	Types of Agreements and Treaties (%)		
	Procedural	Providing Goods	Military
Roosevelt			
First term			
Average for first 3 years	90.7	4.1	5.2
Average for 2nd and 3rd years	89.8	4.3	5.9
Fourth year (election year)	80.4	3.9	15.7
Second term			
Average for first 3 years	86.5	4.8	8.6
Average for 2nd and 3rd years	82.8	4.3	13.0
Fourth year (election year)	71.7	0.0	28.3
Third term			
Average for first 3 years	46.0	14.9	39.1
Average for 2nd and 3rd years	49.2	18.8	32.0
Fourth year (election year)	58.3	27.4	14.3
Truman			
First term			
Average for first 3 years	63.3	21.3	15.4
Average for 2nd and 3rd years	68.7	23.1	8.2
Fourth year (election year)	57.7	37.4	5.0
Second term			
Average for first 3 years	43.5	40.3	16.2
Average for 2nd and 3rd years	34.3	45.6	20.2
Fourth year (election year)	38.7	46.8	14.5
Eisenhower			
First term			
Average for first 3 years	38.3	37.8	23.8

Table 6B–*continues*

Table 6B—*continued*

President, Term, and Year	Types of Agreements and Treaties (%)		
	Procedural	Providing Goods	Military
Average for 2nd and 3rd years	40.2	37.2	22.6
Fourth year (election year)	40.9	41.7	17.3
Johnson First elected term Average for first 3 years	57.2	33.9	8.8
Average for 2nd and 3rd years	58.9	33.4	7.4
Fourth year (election year)	51.9	38.3	9.8
Nixon First term Average for first 3 years	53.5	35.1	11.4
Average for 2nd and 3rd years	56.8	33.1	10.1
Fourth year (election year)	63.2	29.9	6.9

Table 7 Effects of Being in First Year of Presidential Office on Number of Agreements and Treaties Made*

President	First Year	Average for the Other Years	First Year Lowest?
F. Roosevelt	26	67.3 (last year adjusted)	yes
Eisenhower	177	248.3	yes
Kennedy	260	286.2	no
Nixon	171	249.8	yes (if last year is adjusted)
Carter (only 2 years studied)	375	309.0	no

*This table considers only presidents who first came to office by election, not in an unexpected manner.

Table 8 Effect of Coming into Presidential Office Unexpectedly on the Number of Agreements and Treaties Made*

President and Year (Unexpected President and Predecessor)	Number of Agreements and Treaties
Truman	
2 years before FDR's death	99
1 year before FDR's death	89
FDR (Jan. 20-Apr. 12, 1945)	35 (140)
Truman (Apr. 12, 1945-Jan. 20, 1946)	90 (120)
Truman's first full year	163
Truman's second full year	192
Johnson	
2 years before Kennedy's death	260
1 year before Kennedy's death	330
JFK (Jan. 20-Nov. 22, 1963)	202 (242.4)
LBJ (Nov. 22, 1963-Jan. 20, 1964)	30 (180)
Johnson's first full year	224
Johnson's second full year	226
Ford	
2 years before Nixon's resignation	295
1 year before Nixon's resignation	235
Nixon (Jan. 20-Aug. 9, 1974)	150 (257)
Ford (Aug. 9, 1974-Jan. 20, 1975)	105 (252)
Ford's first full year	298
Ford's second full year	370

*This table looks only at presidents who came into office in an unexpected manner, through the death or resignation of their predecessors. The values in parentheses are adjusted values for the shortened presidential years; that is, they represent the number of agreements and treaties that would have been made in a full year based upon the rate at which they were made during the shortened presidential year.

Table 8B "Unexpected" versus "Expected" Presidents: The Types of Agreements Made (in percent)

President	Type of Agreements		
	Procedural	Providing Goods	Military
Unexpected Presidents			
Roosevelt's last full year	58.3	27.4	14.3
Transitional year (FDR-Truman)	50.7	19.9	29.4
Truman's first full year	75.6	19.0	5.4
Kennedy's last full year	37.9	50.0	12.1
Transitional year (JFK-LBJ)	54.1	39.2	6.7
Johnson's first full year	51.3	41.2	7.5
Nixon's last full year	62.6	28.7	8.7
Transitional year (Nixon-Ford)	61.1	33.0	5.9
Ford's first full year	58.3	34.5	7.2
Expected Presidents			
Truman's last year	38.7	46.8	14.5
Eisenhower's first year	34.5	39.1	26.4
Eisenhower's last year	37.1	41.5	21.3
Kennedy's first year	37.4	49.6	13.0
Johnson's last year	51.9	38.3	9.8
Nixon's first year	46.8	39.2	14.0
Ford's last year	50.5	43.9	5.6
Carter's first year	52.7	43.7	3.6

Table 9 "Unexpected" versus "Expected" Presidents: A Comparison of Performance

President and Year	Number of Agreements and Treaties	Increase or Decrease from Previous Year (percentage)
Unexpected Presidents		
Roosevelt's last full year	89	-
Transition year (FDR-Truman)	125	+40.4
Truman's first full year	163	+30.4
Kennedy's last full year	330	-
Transition year (JFK-LBJ)	232	−29.7
Johnson's first full year	224	− 3.4
Nixon's last full year	235	-
Transition year (Nixon-Ford)	255	+ 8.5
Ford's first full year	298	+16.9
Expected (Elected) Presidents		
Truman's last year	270	-
Eisenhower's first year	177	−34.4
Eisenhower's last year	274	-
Kennedy's first year	260	− 5.1
Johnson's last year	186	-
Nixon's first year	171	− 8.1
Ford's last year	370	-
Carter's first year	375	+ 1.4

Table 10 Agreements and Treaties Made with Each Area or Nation in Each Presidential Year*

	Western Europe		USSR		Eastern Europe		Americas**		Africa		Asia		Mexico		Canada	
	No.	%	No.	%	No.	%	No.	%	No.	%	No.	%	No.	%	No.	%
Roosevelt																
1	8	31	1	4			2	8	3	12	1	4	0	0	1	4
2	9	24			6	16	12	32			2	5	2	5	1	3
3	9	28	2	6	5	16	7	22			1	3	2	6	5	16
4	9	18	1	2	3	6	10	20			2	4	1	2	2	4
5	8	22	1	3	4	11	6	17	2	6	3	8	2	6	2	6
6	7	15	1	2	5	11	12	26	2	4	2	4	2	6	8	17
7	10	25			1	3	12	30	2	5	1	3	1	3	6	15
8	5	12					15	36	3	7					11	26
9	4	7					32	53	1	2					11	18
10	19	14	1	1	4	3	45	34	2	1			5	8	16	12
11	10	10			2	2	37	37	4	4	5	5	8	6	11	11
12	16	18					35	39	2	2	6	7	11	11	7	8
13 (short.)	7	20	1	3	1	3	10	29			1	3	4	4	3	9
Truman																
1 (short.)	24	27	4	4	2	2	15	17	4	4	2	2	3	3	4	4
2	47	29	1	1	8	5	28	17	8	5	18	11	1	1	7	4
3	61	32			7	4	38	20	7	4	36	19	5	3	8	4
4	90	40	1	0	3	1	47	21	2	1	32	14	1	0	6	3
5	49	21			1	0	59	25	5	2	29	12	14	6	8	3
6	43	25			7	4	64	37	4	2	31	18	2	1	6	3
7	66	25			3	1	96	37	8	3	48	18	5	2	7	3
8	58	21			3	1	80	30	20	7	56	21	8	3	7	3

Table 10–*continues*

Table 10—*continued*

	Western Europe		USSR		Eastern Europe		Americas**		Africa		Asia		Mexico		Canada	
	No.	%	No.	%	No.	%	No.	%	No.	%	No.	%	No.	%	No.	%
Eisenhower																
1	46	26			3	2	36	20	20	11	38	21	3	2	7	4
2	55	25	2	1	3	1	46	21	11	5	59	27	10	5	6	3
3	77	24	3	1	10	3	109	34	14	4	67	21	2	1	9	3
4	68	27			3	1	54	21	7	3	76	30	2	1	10	4
5	65	31			6	3	47	22	13	6	57	26	8	4	1	0
6	49	23	2	1	12	6	36	17	10	5	60	29	4	2	3	1
7	50	20	1	0	7	3	51	21	14	6	76	31	8	3	8	3
8	67	24			9	3	58	21	17	6	78	28	4	1	7	3
Kennedy																
1	49	19	1	0	8	3	48	18	30	12	75	29	8	3	10	4
2	58	18	1	0	8	2	79	24	43	13	87	26	4	1	7	2
3 (short.)	32	16	1	0	5	2	42	21	21	10	64	32	5	2	4	2
Johnson																
1 (short.)	4	13					5	17	7	23	7	23	1	3	2	7
2	42	19	4	2	13	6	27	12	30	13	54	24	5	2	8	4

3	37	16	2	1	8	4	29	13	30	13	64	28	5	2	14	6
4	45	19	3	1	3	1	30	13	29	12	76	32	5	2	9	4
5	26	11	5	2	8	3	25	11	34	14	68	29	7	3	12	5
6	28	15	7	4	3	2	37	20	17	9	59	32	4	2	4	2
Nixon																
1	27	16	6	4	6	4	21	12	12	7	57	33	1	1	9	5
2	34	15	5	2	9	4	40	18	15	7	71	31	11	5	8	4
3	24	10	7	3	6	3	42	18	19	8	90	38	5	2	11	5
4	36	12	19	6	12	4	65	22	10	3	96	33	14	5	6	2
5	35	15	21	9	15	6	27	11	8	3	74	31	12	5	11	5
6 (short.)	20	13	6	4	5	3	16	11	13	9	49	33	6	4	7	5
Ford																
1 (short.)	12	11	2	2	7	7	17	16	6	6	33	31	8	8	3	3
2	45	15	13	4	13	4	45	15	25	8	95	32	11	4	11	4
3	40	11	5	1	12	3	76	21	46	12	111	30	18	5	15	4
Carter																
1	38	10	8	2	18	5	43	11	70	19	130	35	18	5	15	4
2	34	11	8	3	17	6	34	11	60	19	101	33	20	6	9	3

*This chart does not include multilateral agreements and treaties or agreements and treaties with international organizations.

**Excepting Mexico.

Table 10B   Ratio of Agreements/Treaties Made with Each Area or Nation in Each Presidential Year

President	Western Europe	USSR	Eastern Bloc	Americas*	Africa	Asia	Mexico	Canada
Roosevelt								
1	8:0	1:0		2:0	3:0	1:0		0:1
2	5:4		2:4	10:1		1:1	0:2	1:0
3	6:3	2:0	3:2	5:2		1:0	0:2	4:1
4	4:5	1:0	2:1	10:0		2:0	0:1	0:2
5	6:2	1:0	3:1	6:0	1:1	2:1	1:1	2:0
6	5:2	1:0	5:0	11:1	0:2	1:1	2:0	7:1
7	6:4		1:0	10:2	1:1	1:0	0:1	6:0
8	4:1			13:2	0:3			10:1
9	4:0			32:0	1:0		3:2	10:1
10	10:0	1:0	5:0	65:0	2:0	3:1	7:1	15:1
11	10:0		2:0	36:0	4:0	6:0	10:0	11:0
12	16:0			34:0	2:0	6:0	3:1	6:1
13	7:0	1:0	1:0	10:0		1:0		3:0
Truman								
1	22:2	4:0	2:0	15:0	4:0	2:0	3:0	4:0
2	46:1	1:0	8:0	27:0	6:2	16:2	1:0	7:0
3	61:0		7:0	36:2	3:4	34:1	5:0	8:0
4	84:6		3:0	47:0	2:0	32:0	1:0	6:0
5	43:6	1:0	1:0	58:1	4:0	29:0	11:3	8:0
6	39:4		7:0	60:4	4:0	31:0	2:0	3:3
7	59:7		3:0	96:0	7:1	45:3	5:0	5:2
8	58:1		3:0	80:0	20:0	56:0	8:0	6:1
Eisenhower								
1	42:4		3:0	42:0	19:0	30:0	3:0	6:1
2	52:3	2:0	3:0	44:0	11:0	57:3	10:0	5:1
3	74:3	3:0	10:0	108:1	14:0	66:1	2:0	9:0
4	65:4		3:0	52:2	7:0	74:1	2:0	8:2
5	64:2		6:0	47:0	12:0	53:0	7:1	1:0
6	48:1	2:0	12:0	35:1	9:0	61:0	4:0	3:0
7	48:2	1:0	7:0	50:0	15:0	76:2	8:0	8:0
8	68:1		10:0	57:1	18:0	74:1	4:0	6:1
Kennedy								
1	50:2	1:0	8:0	48:0	30:0	69:1	8:0	9:1
2	56:2	1:0	8:0	72:0	49:0	81:3	4:0	7:0
3	31:3	1:0	5:0	39:0	24:0	61:1	4:1	4:0
Johnson								
1	4:0			5:0	7:0	7:0	1:0	2:0
2	39:1	3:1	13:0	23:0	34:0	54:0	5:0	8:0
3	35:3	2:0	8:0	27:0	32:0	64:0	5:0	13:1
4	38:2	3:0	3:0	29:1	32:1	75:1	4:1	8:1
5	25:1	5:0	8:0	25:0	34:0	67:0	7:0	11:1
6	30:0	7:0	3:0	37:0	17:0	60:0	3:1	4:0

Table 10B—*continues*

Table 10B—*continued*

President	Western Europe	USSR	Eastern Bloc	Americas*	Africa	Asia	Mexico	Canada
Nixon								
1	25:2	6:0	6:0	18:1	14:0	58:0	1:0	6:3
2	30:4	5:0	8:0	38:1	16:0	71:0	9:2	8:0
3	23:1	7:0	6:0	39:1	22:0	90:2	5:0	9:1
4	33:3	18:1	9:3	62:2	10:1	97:1	14:0	6:0
5	34:1	20:1	14:1	23:1	9:0	75:0	12:0	10:1
6	20:0	5:1	4:1	14:0	16:0	49:0	6:0	7:0
Ford								
1	13:0	2:0	6:1	16:0	6:0	33:0	8:0	3:0
2	40:2	14:0	12:0	44:1	25:0	95:0	11:0	11:0
3	39:1	4:1	12:0	69:0	52:0	111:1	17:1	15:0
Carter								
1	37:1	8:0	18:0	41:0	74:0	129:0	18:0	14:1
2	30:4	8:0	17:0	26:2	62:0	99:1	19:1	9:0

*Excepting Mexico.

Table 11 Percentage of Agreements and Treaties Each President Made with Each Area of the World

President	Western Europe	USSR	Eastern Bloc	Americas*	Africa	Asia	Mexico	Canada
Roosevelt	18.8	1.6	5.5	29.5	3.3	3.5	4.2	11.5
Truman	27.5	0.6	2.3	25.5	3.5	14.4	2.4	3.4
Eisenhower	25.0	0.4	2.8	22.1	5.8	26.6	2.4	2.6
Kennedy	17.7	0.0	2.3	21.0	11.7	29.0	2.0	2.7
Johnson	15.5	1.7	2.7	14.3	14.0	28.0	2.3	4.7
Nixon	13.5	4.7	4.0	15.3	6.2	33.2	3.7	4.3
Ford	12.3	2.3	4.7	17.3	8.6	31.0	5.7	3.7
Carter (2 years)	10.5	2.5	5.5	11.0	19.0	34.0	5.5	3.5

*Excepting Mexico.

Table 11B Ratio of Agreements to Treaties that Each President Made with Each Area of the World

Presidents	Western Europe	USSR	Eastern Bloc	Americas*	Africa	Asia	Mexico	Canada
Roosevelt (13 yrs.)	100:21 (4.8:1)	8:0	24:8 (3:1)	244:8 (30.5:1)	14:7 (2:1)	25:4 (6.3:1)	26:11 (2.4:1)	75:9 (8.3:1)
Truman (8 yrs.)	412:27 (15.3:1)	6:0	34:0	419:7 (59.9:1)	50:7 (7.1:1)	254:6 (40.8:1)	36.3 (12:1)	47:6 (7.8:1)
Eisenhower (8 yrs)	461:20 (23.1:1)	8:0	54:0	435:2 (217.5:1)	105:0	491:11 (44.6:1)	40:1 (40:1)	46:5 (9.2:1)
Kennedy (3 yrs.)	137:7 (19.6:1)	3:0	21:0	159:0	103:0	211:5 (42.2:1)	16:1	20:1
Johnson (6 yrs.)	171:7 (24.4:1)	20:1	35:0	146:1	156:1	327:1	25:2 (12.5:1)	46:3 (15.3:1)
Nixon (6 yrs.)	165:11 (15:1)	61:3 (20.3:1)	47:5 (9.4:1)	194:6 (32.3:1)	87:1	440:3 (146.7:1)	47:2 (23.5:1)	46:5 (9.2:1)
Ford (3 yrs.)	92:3 (30.7:1)	20:1	30:1	129:1	83:0	239:1	36:1	29:0
Carter (2 yrs.)	67:5 (13.4:1)	16:0	35:0	67:2 (33.5:1)	136:0	228:1	37:1	23:1
Composite	1605:101 (15.9:1)	142:5 (28.4:1)	280:14 (20:1)	1793:27 (66.4:1)	734:16 (45.9:1)	2206:32 (68.9:1)	263:22 (11.9:1)	332:30 (11.1:1)

*Excepting Mexico.

Table 12 Effects of Conflict on the Number of Agreements and Treaties Concluded

War or "Police Action" (related year)	Total Agreements and Treaties Made
World War II	
2 years before U.S. entered World War II	42
1 year before U.S. entered World War II	60
First full year that U.S. is at war	134
Second full year	99
Third full year	89
Fourth year	125
The year after World War II ended	163
Second full year after World War II ended	192
Korean War	
2 years before war began	223
1 year before war began	236
The year that the U.S. entered (in July)	173
First full year that the U.S. is at war	263
Second full year	270
Third year (peace is concluded at mid-year)	177
First full year of peace	218
Second full year of peace	321
Vietnam	
2 years before the U.S. became deeply involved in Vietnam	330
1 year before	232
The year of the Gulf of Tonkin Resolution	224
The following year	226
The following year	238
The following year	236
The following year	186
The following year	171
The following year	226
The following year	236
The following year	295
1973; U.S. pulled its troops out of Vietnam (U.S. still arming South Vietnam)	235
1974; the U.S. is still arming South Vietnam	255
1975; Vietnam falls in April	298
The year after Vietnam (South Vietnam) fell	370
Two years after	375

Table 12B Effects of Conflict on the Types of Agreements Made

War or "Police Action" (related year)	Types of Agreements		
	Procedural	Goods	Military
World War II			
2 years before U.S. entered World War II	71.7	0.0	28.3
1 year before	39.7	6.9	53.4
First full year that U.S. is at war	52.9	17.1	30.0
Second full year	45.4	20.6	34.0
Third full year	58.3	27.4	14.3
Fourth year at war	50.7	19.9	29.4
Year after World War II ended	75.6	19.0	5.4
Second full year after war ended	61.8	27.1	11.1
Korean War			
2 years before U.S. entered the war	57.7	37.4	5.0
1 year before	62.0	29.7	8.3
Year that the U.S. entered the war (in July)	42.4	39.0	18.6
First full year that the U.S. is in the war	26.1	52.1	21.8
Second full year	38.7	46.8	14.5
Third year of war (peace concluded at mid-year)	34.5	39.1	26.4
First full year of peace	43.1	31.2	25.7
Second full year	37.3	43.2	19.4
Vietnam			
2 years before U.S. became deeply involved in Vietnam	37.9	50.0	12.1
1 year before U.S. became deeply involved in Vietnam	54.1	39.2	6.8
The year of the Gulf of Tonkin Resolution	51.3	41.2	7.5
The following year	53.9	34.2	11.8
The following year	52.7	39.3	7.9
The following year	65.0	28.2	6.8
The following year	51.9	38.3	9.8
The following year	46.8	39.2	14.0
The following year	61.3	28.9	9.8
The following year	52.3	37.3	10.4
The following year (U.S. still deeply involved)	63.2	29.9	6.9
1973; U.S. pulled troops out of Vietnam (still arming South Vietnam)	62.6	28.7	8.7
1974; U.S. is still arming South Vietnam	61.1	33.0	5.9
1975; Vietnam falls in April	58.3	34.5	7.2
The year after South Vietnam fell	50.5	43.9	5.6
Two years after	52.7	43.7	3.6

Table 13 The Top Ten Nations with Whom the Most Agreements and Treaties
Were Concluded in Each Presidential Year

Presidential Year and Nation	Number of Agreements	Number of Treaties	Total
Roosevelt: First Year of Term			
Sweden	3	0	3
Norway	3	0	3
Haiti	2	0	2
South Africa	2	0	2
Canada	0	1	1
France	1	0	1
Finland	0	1	1
Ireland	1	0	1
Saudi Arabia	1	0	1
Egypt	1	0	1
USSR	1	0	1
Roosevelt: Second Year of Term			
Brazil	3	0	3
Denmark	3	0	3
Lithuania	1	1	2
Mexico	0	2	2
Panama	2	0	2
Argentina	1	0	1
Austria	0	1	1
Belgium	1	0	1
(15 other nations had 1)			
Roosevelt: Third Year of Term			
Canada	4	1	5
Belgium	1	1	2
Czechoslovakia	1	1	2
Mexico	0	2	2
Panama	0	2	2
Poland	1	1	2
United Kingdom	2	0	2
USSR	2	0	2
(11 nations had 1)			
Roosevelt: Fourth Year of Term			
France	3	1	4
Canada	0	2	2
Ecuador	2	0	2
Hungary	2	0	2
(19 nations had 1)			
Roosevelt: Fifth Year of Term			
Canada	2	0	2
Chile	2	0	2
Ireland	2	0	2
Lithuania	1	1	2
Mexico	1	1	2
(18 nations had 1)			

Table 13—*continues*

Table 13—*Continued*

Presidential Year and Nation	Number of Agreements	Number of Treaties	Total
Roosevelt: Sixth Year of Term			
Canada	7	1	8
Chile	2	0	2
Colombia	2	0	2
Cuba	2	0	2
Czechoslovakia	2	0	2
Finland	1	1	2
France	2	0	2
Iraq	1	1	2
Liberia	0	2	2
Mexico	2	0	2
Roosevelt: Seventh Year of Term			
Canada	6	0	6
France	2	1	3
Sweden	2	1	3
Argentina	2	0	2
Guatemala	1	1	2
Liberia	1	1	2
Nicaragua	2	0	2
Panama	2	0	2
United Kingdom	1	1	2
(10 nations had 1)			
Roosevelt: Eighth Year of Term			
Canada	10	1	11
Brazil	3	0	3
Ecuador	2	0	2
Panama	2	0	2
Peru	2	0	2
United Arab Republic	0	2	2
United Kingdom	2	0	2
(11 nations had 1)			
Roosevelt: Ninth Year of Term			
Canada	10	1	11
Haiti	6	0	6
Mexico	3	2	5
Costa Rica	4	0	4
Bolivia	2	0	2
Cuba	2	0	2
Dominican Republic	2	0	2
Ecuador	2	0	2
El Salvador	2	0	2
Iceland	2	0	2
Nicaragua	2	0	2
Panama	2	0	2
Roosevelt: Tenth Year of Term			
Canada	15	1	16
Brazil	9	0	9

Table 13—*continues*

Table 13—*Continued*

Presidential Year and Nation	Number of Agreements	Number of Treaties	Total
United Kingdom	9	0	9
Mexico	7	1	8
Haiti	7	0	7
Peru	7	0	7
Ecuador	7	0	7
Nicaragua	5	0	5
Colombia	4	0	4
El Salvador	4	0	4
Roosevelt: Eleventh Year of Term			
Canada	11	0	11
Mexico	10	0	10
United Kingdom	5	0	5
Brazil	4	0	4
Dominican Republic	4	0	4
El Salvador	4	0	4
Panama	4	0	4
Chile	3	0	3
Iran	3	0	3
Venezuela	3	0	3
Roosevelt: Twelfth Year of Term			
Peru	8	0	8
Canada	6	1	7
Haiti	5	0	5
France	4	0	4
Guatemala	4	0	4
Mexico	3	1	4
Brazil	3	0	3
(8 nations had 2)			
Roosevelt: Thirteenth Year			
(Jan. 20-Apr. 12, 1945)			
Canada	3	0	3
Peru	3	0	3
Ecuador	2	0	2
France	2	0	2
Guatemala	2	0	2
Iceland	2	0	2
Norway	2	0	2
(10 nations had 1)			
Truman: First Year			
(Apr. 12, 1945-Jan. 20, 1946)			
United Kingdom	5	2	7
Haiti	5	0	5
Canada	4	0	4
USSR	4	0	4
Chile	3	0	3
France	3	0	3
Italy	3	0	3
Mexico	3	0	3
(6 nations had 2)			

Table 13—*continues*

Table 13—*Continued*

Presidential Year and Nation	Number of Agreements	Number of Treaties	Total
Truman: Second Year of Term			
France	9	1	10
United Kingdom	10	0	10
Canada	7	0	7
Brazil	6	0	6
Philippines	5	1	6
Belgium	5	0	5
Peru	5	0	5
Poland	5	0	5
China (Taiwan)	3	1	4
Portugal	4	0	4
United Arab Republic	4	0	4
Truman: Third Year of Term			
Philippines	18	1	19
France	15	0	15
United Kingdom	12	0	12
Canada	8	0	8
Haiti	6	0	6
Italy	6	0	6
Netherlands	6	0	6
South Africa	2	4	6
Austria	5	0	5
Bolivia	5	0	5
China (Taiwan)	5	0	5
Ecudaor	5	0	5
Mexico	5	0	5
Peru	5	0	5
Truman: Fourth Year of Term			
France	17	1	18
Italy	12	1	13
Philippines	12	0	12
United Kingdom	11	0	11
Belgium	7	2	9
Bolivia	6	0	6
Brazil	6	0	6
Canada	6	0	6
China (Taiwan)	6	0	6
Paraguay	6	0	6
Truman: Fifth Year of Term			
Mexico	11	3	14
United Kingdom	9	0	9
Canada	8	0	8
Philippines	8	0	8
Ecuador	6	0	6
Korea	6	0	6
Norway	3	3	6
Panama	6	0	6
Chile	5	0	5

Table 13—*continues*

Table 13—*Continued*

Presidential Year and Nation	Number of Agreements	Number of Treaties	Total
Colombia	5	0	5
Greece	5	0	5
Haiti	5	0	5
Peru	5	0	5
Truman: Sixth Year of Term			
Brazil	9	0	9
Panama	3	4	7
Peru	7	0	7
Canada	3	3	6
Chile	6	0	6
United Kingdom	6	0	6
Yugoslavia	6	0	6
Costa Rica	5	0	5
Korea	5	0	5
Paraguay	5	0	5
Truman: Seventh Year of Term			
United Kingdom	11	1	12
Italy	8	1	9
El Salvador	8	0	8
Honduras	8	0	8
Canada	5	2	7
Cuba	7	0	7
Nicaragua	7	0	7
Paraguay	7	0	7
Bolivia	6	0	6
Ecuador	6	0	6
France	6	0	6
Panama	6	0	6
Truman: Eighth Year of Term			
Iraq	10	0	10
Israel	9	0	9
Brazil	8	0	8
Chile	8	0	8
El Salvador	8	0	8
Libya	8	0	8
Mexico	8	0	8
Canada	6	1	7
France	7	0	7
Saudi Arabia	7	0	7
United Kingdom	7	0	7
Eisenhower: First Year of Term			
Germany	7	4	11
Ethiopia	10	0	10
Belgium	7	0	7
Canada	6	1	7
Cuba	6	0	6
El Salvador	6	0	6

Table 13—*continues*

Table 13—*Continued*

Presidential Year and Nation	Number of Agreements	Number of Treaties	Total
United Kingdom	6	0	6
Chile	5	0	5
Egypt	5	0	5
Japan	5	0	5
Pakistan	5	0	5
Eisenhower; Second Year of Term			
Japan	13	2	15
Mexico	10	0	10
Pakistan	10	0	10
Germany	7	2	9
Canada	5	1	6
Italy	6	0	6
Norway	6	0	6
Peru	6	0	6
United Kingdom	5	1	6
(6 nations had 5)			
Eisenhower: Third Year of Term			
Italy	11	2	13
Germany	11	0	11
Peru	11	0	11
Ecuador	10	0	10
Haiti	10	0	10
Yugoslavia	10	0	10
Brazil	9	0	9
Canada	9	0	9
Colombia	9	0	9
Libya	9	0	9
Turkey	9	0	9
United Kingdom	9	0	9
Eisenhower: Fourth Year of Term			
Japan	14	0	14
Spain	11	0	11
Canada	8	2	10
Germany	10	0	10
France	8	1	9
Pakistan	9	0	9
Peru	9	0	9
United Kingdom	9	0	9
China (Taiwan)	8	0	8
Korea	6	1	7
Turkey	7	0	7
Eisenhower: Fifth Year of Term			
United Kingdom	10	1	11
Germany	8	0	8
Italy	8	0	8
Japan	7	1	8

Table 13—*continues*

Table 13—*Continued*

Presidential Year and Nation	Number of Agreements	Number of Treaties	Total
Mexico	7	1	8
Brazil	6	0	6
Colombia	6	0	6
Greece	6	0	6
Iran	6	0	6
Peru	6	0	6
Philippines	6	0	6
Spain	6	0	6
Eisenhower: Sixth Year of Term			
Philippines	10	0	10
Spain	9	0	9
France	8	0	8
Japan	8	0	8
United Kingdom	8	0	8
Yugoslavia	8	0	8
Brazil	6	0	6
Turkey	6	0	6
(7 nations had 5)			
Eisenhower: Seventh Year of Term			
Turkey	12	0	12
Japan	8	1	9
Canada	8	0	8
India	8	0	8
Mexico	8	0	8
Germany	7	0	7
Pakistan	6	1	7
Brazil	6	0	6
China (Taiwan)	6	0	6
Colombia	6	0	6
France	5	1	6
United Arab Republic	6	0	6
Eisenhower: Eighth Year of Term			
Brazil	11	1	12
Chile	12	0	12
Korea	10	0	10
China (Taiwan)	9	0	9
Italy	9	0	9
Japan	8	1	9
United Kingdom	9	0	9
Canada	6	1	7
India	7	0	7
Norway	7	0	7
Peru	7	0	7
United Arab Republic	7	0	7
Kennedy: First Year of Term			
Canada	9	1	10
Pakistan	10	0	10

Table 13—*continues*

Table 13—*Continued*

Presidential Year and Nation	Number of Agreements	Number of Treaties	Total
United Kingdom	10	0	10
Turkey	9	0	9
Brazil	8	0	8
Colombia	8	0	8
Mexico	8	0	8
Germany	7	0	7
Greece	7	0	7
France	6	0	6
(4 other nations had 6)			
Kennedy: Second Year of Term			
China (Taiwan)	10	0	10
Japan	9	1	10
United Kingdom	10	0	10
Israel	8	1	9
Germany	8	0	8
India	8	0	8
United Arab Republic	8	0	8
Brazil	7	0	7
Canada	7	0	7
Congo	7	0	7
Korea	6	1	7
Kennedy: Third Year of Term (Jan. 20-Nov. 22, 1963)			
Japan	9	1	10
India	8	0	8
Korea	6	0	6
United Kingdom	6	0	6
Australia	5	0	5
Belgium	4	1	5
Bolivia	5	0	5
Israel	5	0	5
Mexico	4	1	5
Paraguay	5	0	5
Philippines	5	0	5
Johnson: First Year of Term (Nov. 22, 1963-Jan. 20, 1964)			
Brazil	2	0	2
Canada	2	0	2
China (Taiwan)	2	0	2
Colombia	2	0	2
Somali Republic	2	0	2
(17 nations had 1)			
Johnson: Second Year of Term			
China (Taiwan)	10	0	10
Yugoslavia	10	0	10
Canada	8	0	8
Greece	6	1	7

Table 13—*continues*

Table 13—*Continued*

Presidential Year and Nation	Number of Agreements	Number of Treaties	Total
India	7	0	7
Iceland	6	0	6
Spain	6	0	6
United Kingdom	6	0	6
(6 nations had 5)			
Johnson: Third Year of Term			
Canada	13	1	14
Philippines	12	0	12
Vietnam	8	0	8
Brazil	7	0	7
Japan	7	0	7
Yugoslavia	7	0	7
India	6	0	6
China (Taiwan)	5	0	5
Israel	5	0	5
Italy	5	0	5
Mexico	5	0	5
United Kingdom	5	0	5
Johnson: Fourth Year of Term			
United Kingdom	10	1	11
Canada	8	1	9
India	9	0	9
Philippines	9	0	9
Indonesia	6	0	6
Korea	6	0	6
Pakistan	6	0	6
Vietnam	6	0	6
Israel	5	0	5
Japan	5	0	5
Mexico	5	0	5
Paraguay	5	0	5
Spain	5	0	5
Johnson: Fifth Year of Term			
Canada	11	1	12
Japan	9	0	9
Philippines	9	0	9
Indonesia	8	0	8
Brazil	7	0	7
India	7	0	7
Mexico	7	0	7
China (Taiwan)	6	0	6
Pakistan	6	0	6
United Kingdom	6	0	6
Vietnam	6	0	6

Table 13—*continues*

Table 13—*Continued*

Presidential Year and Nation	Number of Agreements	Number of Treaties	Total
Johnson: Sixth Year of Term			
Japan	8	0	8
Colombia	7	0	7
Indonesia	7	0	7
USSR	7	0	7
Vietnam	6	0	6
Brazil	5	0	5
Israel	5	0	5
Korea	5	0	5
Philippines	5	0	5
(5 nations had 4)			
Nixon: First Year of Term			
Vietnam	10	0	10
Canada	6	3	9
Japan	8	0	8
USSR	6	0	6
Turkey	5	0	5
Afghanistan	4	0	4
China (Taiwan)	4	0	4
Indonesia	4	0	4
Iran	4	0	4
Pakistan	4	0	4
Philippines	4	0	4
Spain	4	0	4
Nixon: Second Year of Term			
Mexico	9	2	11
Vietnam	11	0	11
Indonesia	10	0	10
Canada	8	0	8
Japan	6	0	6
Philippines	6	0	6
China (Taiwan)	5	0	5
Korea	5	0	5
Spain	4	1	5
USSR	5	0	5
Nixon: Third Year of Term			
Korea	19	0	19
Canada	9	1	10
Indonesia	9	0	9
USSR	7	0	7
Cambodia	6	0	6
Japan	4	2	6
Philippines	6	0	6
Vietnam	6	0	6
(6 nations had 5)			

Table 13—*continues*

Table 13—*Continued*

Presidential Year and Nation	Number of Agreements	Number of Treaties	Total
Nixon: Fourth Year of Term			
USSR	18	1	19
Mexico	14	0	14
Korea	13	0	13
Japan	11	1	12
Pakistan	12	0	12
Vietnam	11	0	11
United Kingdom	7	1	8
Argentina	5	1	6
Brazil	5	1	6
Canada	6	0	6
China (Taiwan)	6	0	6
Nixon: Fifth Year of Term			
USSR	20	1	21
Mexico	12	0	12
Canada	10	1	11
(North) Vietnam	11	0	11
Pakistan	8	0	8
Japan	7	0	7
Bangladesh	6	0	6
Germany	6	0	6
(5 nations had 5)			
Nixon: Sixth Year of Term (Jan. 20-Aug. 9, 1974)			
Canada	7	0	7
Vietnam	7	0	7
USSR	5	1	6
Egypt	6	0	6
Mexico	6	0	6
Germany	5	0	5
Japan	5	0	5
Bangladesh	4	0	4
Philippines	4	0	4
(4 nations had 3)			
Ford: First Year of Term (Aug. 9, 1974-Jan. 20, 1975)			
Mexico	8	0	8
Bangladesh	5	0	5
Poland	4	1	5
Vietnam	4	0	4
Canada	3	0	3
Egypt	3	0	3
Israel	3	0	3
Japan	3	0	3
Jordan	3	0	3
Korea	3	0	3

Table 13—*continues*

Table 13–*Continued*

Presidential Year and Nation	Number of Agreements	Number of Treaties	Total
Ford: Second Year of Term			
USSR	13	0	13
Egypt	12	0	12
Canada	11	0	11
Mexico	11	0	11
Japan	9	0	9
Iran	8	0	8
Korea	8	0	8
United Kingdom	7	1	8
Chile	7	0	7
Germany	7	0	7
Portugal	7	0	7
Ford: Third Year of Term			
Egypt	20	0	20
Mexico	17	1	18
Canada	15	0	15
Brazil	12	0	12
Colombia	12	0	12
Korea	10	1	11
Pakistan	11	0	11
Bangladesh	10	0	10
Israel	10	0	10
Indonesia	9	0	9
Jordan	9	0	9
Philippines	9	0	9
Carter: First Year of Term			
Egypt	29	0	29
Mexico	18	0	18
Canada	14	1	15
Japan	14	0	14
Korea	10	0	10
Pakistan	9	0	9
Philippines	9	0	9
Germany	8	0	8
Iran	8	0	8
Israel	8	0	8
Jordan	8	0	8
Carter: Second Year of Term			
Mexico	19	1	20
Egypt	18	0	18
Philippines	13	0	13
Indonesia	12	0	12
Canada	9	0	9
United Kingdom	8	1	9

Table 13–*continues*

Table 13–*Continued*

Presidential Year and Nation	Number of Agreements	Number of Treaties	Total
Australia	8	0	8
Japan	7	1	8
Saudi Arabia	8	0	8
Bangladesh	7	0	7
India	7	0	7
USSR	7	0	7

B. EXECUTIVE AGREEMENTS WITH MEXICO AND EGYPT MADE BY PRESIDENT CARTER DURING SECOND YEAR IN OFFICE

In his second year in office (January 20, 1978-January 20, 1979), President Carter made 19 agreements with Mexico and 18 with Egypt. Most of these appear below by title and with a short description.

MEXICO

Title	Description
Narcotic Drugs	U.S. promises to pay for and train Mexican helicopter pilots to help stop the drug traffic.
Narcotic Drugs	U.S. promises to pay for the computerization of information regarding the drug traffic (for the Mexican government).
Narcotic Drugs	U.S. promises to supplement the salaries of Mexican officials who are involved in stopping the drug traffic.
Narcotic Drugs	U.S. will provide eight aircraft to help the Mexican government stop the drug traffic between the two nations.
Narcotic Drugs	U.S. will provide Mexico with technical equipment to help find illicit crops being grown.
Narcotic Drugs	U.S. will provide communications equipment to help Mexico stop the drug traffic.
Narcotic Drugs	U.S. will provide more money—$700,000 —to help Mexico stop the drug traffic.
Narcotic Drugs	U.S. provides Mexico with a contract administration adviser to help in drug operations.
Narcotic Drugs	U.S. will provide equipment and funding to Mexico to help stop the drug traffic.
Environmental Cooperation	The United States and Mexico will cooperate with respect to environmental problems.

Narcotic Drugs	U.S. will provide a technician to aid Mexico with technical equipment with which to stop the drug traffic.
Emergency Deliveries of Water	U.S. will continue giving emergency deliveries of water to Tijuana.
Criminal Investigations	U.S. and Mexico will share information on International Telephone and Telegraph Company to aid a Mexican criminal investigation.
Tourism	Each nation will encourage travel promotion offices to encourage travel between the two nations.

EGYPT

Agricultural Commodities	U.S. agrees to sell agricultural commodities to Egypt.
Exhibition of Art Treasures	U.S. will show the "treasures of Tutankhamun" in San Francisco.
Narcotic Drugs	The two nations agree to cooperate to stop the flow of illegal drugs.
Exhibition of Art Treasures	The U.S. may show the Nubian art treasures.
National Energy Control Center	The Agency for International Development (a U.S. organization) will lend Egypt money for energy development.
Criminal Investigations	Both nations agree to mutual assistance with respect to matters relating to Westinghouse Electric Corporation.
Technical and Feasibility Studies	U.S. creates an organization to help create projects for Agency for International Development funding.
Commodity Import Program	AID agrees to lend Egypt money for motor vehicles.
Economic Assistance	AID agrees to loan money to Egypt.
Economic, Technical, and Related Assistance	U.S. agrees to give these things to Egypt.
Development Planning Studies	U.S. will establish and help fund an Institute of Technological Planning for Egypt.
Integrated Social Work Centers	AID will provide and help fund the building of housing for Egypt.

Housing Upgrading for Low Income Egyptians	AID will help fund the building of housing for Egypt.
Industrial Production	AID grants money to Egypt to develop industry.
Industrial Production	AID loans money to Egypt to develop industry.
Aquaculture Development	U.S. gives Egypt money to help with the improvement of farm fishing.

Source: U.S. Department of State, *U.S. Treaties and Other International Agreements* (Washington, D.C., 1950-present).

C. TWO EXECUTIVE AGREEMENTS

EXCHANGE OF NOTES: HULL-LOTHIAN BASES-DESTROYERS AGREEMENT, 1940

The British Ambassador (Lothian) to the U.S. Secretary of State (Hull):

British Embassy,
Washington, D.C.
September 2nd, 1940

Sir,

I have the honour under instructions from His Majesty's Principle Secretary of State for Foreign Affairs to inform you that in view of the friendly and sympathetic interest of his Majesty's Government in the United Kingdom in the national security of the United States and their desire to strengthen the ability of the United States to cooperate effectively with the other nations of the Americas in the defence of the Western Hemisphere, His Majesty's Government will secure the grant to the Government of the United States, freely and without consideration, of the lease for immediate establishment and use of naval and air bases and facilities for entrance thereto and the operation and protection thereof, on the Avalon Peninsula and on the southern coast of Newfoundland, and on the east coast and on the Great Bay of Bermuda.

Furthermore, in view of the above and in view of the desire of the United States to acquire additional air and naval bases in the Caribbean and in British Guiana, and without endeavouring to place a monetary or commercial value upon the many tangible and intangible rights and properties involved, His Majesty's Government will make available to the United States for immediate establishment and use naval and air bases and facilities for entrance thereto and the operation and protection thereof, on the eastern side of the Bahamas, the southern coast of Jamaica, the western coast of St. Lucia, the west coast of Trinidad in the Gulf of Paria, in the island of Antigua and in British Guiana within fifty miles of Georgetown, in exchange for naval and military equipment and material which the United States Government will transfer to His Majesty's Government.

All the bases and facilities referred to in the preceding paragraphs will be leased to the United States for a period of ninety-nine years, free from all rent and charges other than such compensation to be mutually agreed on to be paid by the United States in order to compensate the owners of private property for loss by expropriation or damage arising out of the establishment of the bases and facilities in question.

His Majesty's Government, in the leases to be agreed upon, will grant to the United States for the period of the leases all the rights, power, and authority within the bases leased, and within the limits of the territorial waters and air spaces adjacent to or in the vicinity of such bases, necessary to provide access to and defence of such bases, and appropriate provisions for their control.

Without prejudice to the above-mentioned rights of the United States authorities and their jurisdiction within the leased areas, the adjustment and reconciliation between the jurisdiction of the authorities of the United States within these areas and the jurisdiction of the authorities of the territories in which these areas are situated, shall be determined by common agreement.

The exact location and bounds of the aforesaid bases, the necessary seaward, coast and anti-aircraft defences, the location of sufficient military garrisons, stores and other necessary auxiliary facilities shall be determined by common agreement.

His Majesty's Government are prepared to designate immediately experts to meet with experts of the United States for these purposes. Should these experts be unable to agree in any particular situation, except in the case of Newfoundland and Bermuda, the matter shall be settled by the Secretary of State of the United States and His Majesty's Secretary of State for Foreign Affairs.

I have the honour to be, with the highest consideration, Sir,
Your most obedient, humble servant,

Lothian

The Honourable Cordell Hull,
Secretary of State of the United States,
Washington, D.C.

The U.S. Secretary of State (Hull) to the British Ambassador (Lothian):

Department of State
Washington
September 2, 1940

Excellency:

I have received your note of September 2, 1940, of which the text is as follows:

[Here the text of the preceding letter was quoted verbatim.]

I am directed by the President to reply to your note as follows:

The Government of the United States appreciates the declaration and the generous action of His Majesty's Government as contained in your communication which are destined to enhance the national security of the United States and greatly to strengthen its ability to cooperate effectively with the other nations of the Americas in the defense of the Western Hemisphere. It therefore gladly accepts the proposals.

The Government of the United States will immediately designate experts to meet with experts designated by His Majesty's Government to determine upon the exact location of the naval and air bases mentioned in your communication under acknowledgment.

In consideration of the declarations above quoted, the Government of the United States will immediately transfer to His Majesty's Government fifty United States Navy Destroyers generally referred to as the twelve hundred-ton type.

Accept, Excellency, the renewed assurances of my highest consideration.

Cordell Hull

His Excellency
The Right Honorable The Marquess of Lothian, C. H.,
British Ambassador.

[*Source*: Elmer Plischke, *Conduct of American Diplomacy* (New York: D. D. Van Nostrand Co., 1950), pp. 485-488.

CONFIRMATION OF ORAL AGREEMENT: MCANINCH-FLORES ON DRUG TRAFFIC, 1978

The U.S. Charge d'Affaires ad interim to the Mexican Attorney General:

August 23, 1978

His Excellency
Licenciado Oscar Flores
Attorney General of the Republic
Mexico 1, D.F.

Dear Mr. Attorney General:

In confirmation of recent conversations between officials of our two Governments relating to the cooperation between Mexico and the United States to curb the illegal traffic in narcotics, I am pleased to advise you that the Government of the United States represented by the Embassy of the United States of America, is willing to enter into additional cooperative arrangements with the Government of Mexico, represented by the Office of the Attorney General, to reduce such traffic.

The Government of the United States agrees to provide eight (8) light helicopters, one (1) cargo aircraft, and funding on an advance or reimbursable basis for the lease of one (1) short-takeoff-and landing (STOL) cargo/passenger aircraft as mutually agreed, together with spare parts and training, at a cost not to exceed Four Million Six Hundred Twenty-Thousand Dollars (US$4,620,000).

The Government of Mexico agrees: To provide and develop means to retain sufficient qualified personnel, as mutually agreed upon, to maximize the availability and utilization of these and other aircraft previously provided by the Government of the United States; to examine the inventory of aircraft devoted to the narcotics program in order to determine which aircraft might be removed from the inventory in the interests of operational efficiency; and to establish a flight training program for pilots of aircraft used in the narcotics program.

It is understood that the provisions of all previous Agreements between the Government of the United States and the Government of Mexico in relation to the narcotics control effort of the Government of Mexico remain in full force and effect, and applicable to this agreement unless otherwise expressly modified herein.

If the foregoing is acceptable to the Government of Mexico, this letter and your reply shall constitute an Agreement between our two Governments.

I take this opportunity to reiterate to you the assurances of my highest consideration and personal esteem.

Vernon D. McAninch
Chargé d'Affaires a.i.

[*Source*: U.S. Department of State, *U.S. Treaties and Other International Agreements* (Washington, D.C., 1950-present).]

BIBLIOGRAPHY

Acheson, Dean. *Present at the Creation*. New York: W. W. Norton and Company, 1969.

Barber, James David. *The Presidential Character*. Englewood Cliffs, N.J.: Prentice-Hall Publishing Company, 1972.

Barnett, James F. "International Agreements without the Advice and Consent of the Senate." *Yale Law Journal* 15 (1905-6).

Bartlett, Ruhl J., ed. *The Record of American Diplomacy*. New York: Alfred A. Knopf, 1948.

Bernstein, Barton J. *Politics and Policies of the Truman Administration*. Chicago: Quadrangle Books, 1970.

Browne, Marjorie Ann. "Executive Agreements and the Congress." The Library of Congress Congressional Research Service Major Issues System. Issue Brief No. IB75035; originated May 1, 1975, updated February 27, 1981.

Burns, James MacGregor. *Roosevelt: The Lion and the Fox*. New York: Harcourt, Brace, and World, 1956.

Cohen, Benjamin, ed. *American Foreign Economic Policy*. New York: Harper and Row, Publishers, 1968.

Corwin, Edward S. *The President's Control of Foreign Relations*. Princeton, N.J.: Princeton University Press, 1917.

Dahl, Robert. *Congress and Foreign Policy*. New York: Harcourt, Brace, and Company, 1950.

DeConde, Alexander, ed. *Encyclopedia of American Foreign Policy*. New York: Charles Scribner's Sons, 1978.

_____, ed. *A History of American Foreign Policy*. New York: Charles Scribner's Sons, 1978.

Fenno, Richard. *Congressmen in Committees*. Boston: Little, Brown and Company, 1973.

Fisher, Louis. *The Constitution Between Friends*. New York: St. Martin's Press, 1978.

_____. "Confidential Funding: A Study of Unvouchered Accounts." Prepared for the House Budget Committee. Washington, D.C.: U.S. Government Printing Office, March 1977.

_____. *Presidential Spending Power*. Princeton, N.J.: Princeton University Press, 1975.

Franck, Thomas M., and Weisband, Edward. *Foreign Policy by Congress*. New York: Oxford University Press, 1979.

Gilbert, Amy. *Executive Agreements and Treaties, 1946-1973*. Endicott, N.Y.: Thomas-Newell, 1973.

Grassmuck, George. *Sectional Biases in Congress on Foreign Policy*. Baltimore, Md.: Johns Hopkins University Press, 1951.

Hamilton, Alexander; Madison, James; and Jay, John. *The Federalist Papers*. Introduction by Clinton Rossiter. New York: New American Library, 1961.

Ingram, Timothy H. "The Billions in the White House Basement." *The Washington Monthly*, January 1972.

Krasner, Stephen D. *Defending the National Interest*. Princeton, N.J.: Princeton University Press, 1978.

McClure, Wallace. *International Executive Agreements*. New York: Columbia University Press, 1941.

Plischke, Elmer. *Conduct of American Diplomacy*. New York: D. D. Van Nostrand Co., 1950.

Porter, Gareth, ed. *Vietnam: The Definitive Documentation of Human Decisions*. 2 vols. Stanfordville, N.Y.: Earl M. Coleman Enterprises, Inc., Publishers, 1979.

Schlesinger, Arthur, Jr. *The Imperial Presidency*. Boston: Houghton Mifflin Company, 1973.

U.S. Congress. *How the United States Finances Its Share of Contributions to NATO*. Report to Congress by the Comptroller General of the U.S., 1973.

————. *U.S. Assistance for the Economic Development of the Republic of Korea*. Report to Congress by the Comptroller General of the United States, July 12, 1973.

U.S. Congress. House. *Hearings before the Subcommittees of the House Appropriations Committee, on Supplemental Appropriations* (pt. 2). 93rd Congress, 2nd session, 1974.

————. *Hearings before the Subcommittees of the House Appropriations Committee, on Supplemental Appropriations for Fiscal Year 1977*. 95th Congress, 1st session, 1977.

U.S. Congress. Senate. *Hearings before the Senate Appropriations Committee, on Supplemental Appropriations for Fiscal Year 1976*. 94th Congress, 2nd session, 1976.

————. *Hearings before the Senate Foreign Relations Committee, on Supplemental Foreign Assistance Authorizations*. 91st Congress, 2nd session, December 11, 1970.

U.S. General Accounting Office. "U.S. Security and Military Assistance: Programs and Related Activities." *Report*, June 1, 1982.

U.S. Department of State. *United States Treaties and Other International Agreements Series*. Vols. 1950-present.

Wood, Gordon S. *The Creation of the American Republic, 1776-1787*. Chapel Hill, N.C.: University of North Carolina Press, 1969.

Yanaga, Chitoshi. *Japan Since Perry*. New York: McGraw-Hill Book Company, 1949.

INDEX

ABOUT THE AUTHOR

Larry Margolis grew up in the small West Texas town of Big Spring. He attended the University of Texas, where he received his B.A. in 1976. His Ph.D. was granted by the University of Michigan in 1984. Dr. Margolis taught at Olivet College, Wittenberg University and he is presently teaching at Illinois State University. Dr. Margolis has taught courses in U.S. politics, Soviet politics, Middle Eastern politics, and the politics of developing nations.

DATE DUE

AUG 7 '87			